ALLERTON PARK INSTITUTE

Number 30

Papers Presented at the Allerton Park Institute

Sponsored by

University of Illinois
Graduate School of Library and Information Science

held

November 6-9, 1988
Chancellor Hotel and Convention Center
Champaign, Illinois

Conserving and Preserving Materials in Nonbook Formats

KATHRYN LUTHER HENDERSON
WILLIAM T HENDERSON

Editors

University of Illinois
Graduate School of Library and Information Science
Urbana-Champaign, Illinois

CONTENTS

Introduction

The thirtieth Allerton Institute was the second in the three decades of these Institutes to be devoted wholly to preservation of library materials. The first with this theme was the twenty-seventh Institute in 1981. In that conference, all but one paper dealt with paper-based materials. In that lone paper, Gerald D. Gibson covered preservation problems of "film, sound recordings, tapes, computer records, and other nonpaper materials" (Gibson, 1981, pp. 89-110). In his introduction, Gibson noted the difficulty he had experienced in covering the problems of each of these formats in one paper and hinted that each could well have formed the content of a discrete paper, so the germ of the idea for the 1988 conference came from Gibson's 1981 remark. In the intervening years, much effort has gone into identifying preservation needs and a great deal of attention has been given to paper preservation. Of course, many problems still remain in these areas; however, considerable progress has been made, especially in the realization that many other institutions share preservation problems with libraries. Meanwhile, the growing collections of nonbook materials in archives, museums, and libraries have increasingly shown the need to focus on the preservation problems of these formats. Each format has its own special conservation and preservation problems; yet, many formats are paper-based or have components that contain paper and are, therefore, also subject to all the problems related to paper. Some formats require special equipment which may become obsolete or present other preservation difficulties. This conference addressed the care and preservation of a wide range of nonbook materials and attempted to accomplish the following five general goals and purposes: (1) to identify issues and problems related to the preservation of nonbook materials; (2) to examine different

1

methods and techniques used in the care and preservation of these materials; (3) to provide perspectives on research activities and future trends in nonbook preservation; (4) to indicate the role of vendors and suppliers in the preservation process; and (5) to suggest ways of utilizing strategic planning in the preservation process.

At the conference, the presentations were marked by strong emphases on identifying issues, examining different methods and techniques, describing research activities (or their lack), and predicting future trends. Two presenters each dealt specifically with a particular goal listed above: a vendor described the role of his firm while a library preservation specialist discussed the place of strategic planning for preservation in a library environment. Most speakers utilized slides to illustrate their oral presentations; unfortunately, these cannot be reproduced in the printed proceedings. Thus, only those in attendance were able to share fully in the richness added by these visual enhancements. Also, only those in attendance could be a part of the lively question-and-answer sessions and the meal conversations in which participants continued the discussions begun in the formal sessions.

This was truly the "ecumenical" conference that we had hoped it would be, not only in the selection of speakers who work in libraries, archives, and museums but also because those who attended the conference came from libraries, archives, museums, historical associations, conservation agencies, library and information schools, and the vendor community. They came from many places in the United States; some came from Canada and one came from Venezuela. It soon became apparent that the 130 participants were one in spirit and that preservation needs are not institution or area bound.

In the first paper from the conference, Lambertus van Zelst assesses the needs and accomplishments of preservation in libraries, archives, and museums basing this assessment upon a graph prepared by the National Institute for the Conservation of Cultural Property. Factors relating to public information, professional information, professional training, research, and preventive care and treatment are covered in this assessment, along with the detailing of the work of many national and international organizations engaged in preservation activities, education, and research. In essence, van Zelst describes this ongoing activity as "a field in motion." There are great needs and difficulties, but there is also active progress along with many promises for a successful future as challenges are met. He is optimistic about the future as numerous institutions continue to work together.

Vendors play an important role in preservation. Dennis Inch discusses the responsibilities of vendors, the range of supplies needed to care for a photographic collection, and some of the problems encountered in providing a safe storage environment for photographs. He concludes by relating how one vendor, Light Impressions, keeps current on the changing field of photographic preservation.

At this conference, Gerald D. Gibson had the opportunity to report on only one type of format rather than the several required of him in 1981. He describes the low level of independent research into the problems of recorded sound and assesses preservation practices based on years of experience. He deals primarily with the more common recording media—cylinders, discs, and tapes—pointing out areas in particular need of solid information and reporting on those practices which shape major preservation efforts. He also notes the problems of obsolete equipment. Gibson's paper concludes with several appendices which summarize basic information on the more common recording media and which present, in capsule form, basic information on accepted storage and preservation procedures.

Gordon B. Neavill treats the preservation problems of computer-based and computer-generated materials in a paper which may be one of the more significant conference presentations for identifying future concerns. He sketches the historical context from which computer materials have sprung, describes some of the more significant studies and consultative efforts dealing with preservation of computer-related materials, and explores the preservation problems and prospects of each of a number of data storage media together with the question of the obsolescence of computer hardware as a preservation factor. In his description of the problems facing the information professions in attempting to preserve computer-related materials, Neavill sees great difficulties and indicates that the situation is not unlike that which existed when printing was in its infancy. The need is for a mechanism or combination of mechanisms which will be effective in transmitting information both through space and time. Paper has done both fairly effectively. How both are to be achieved for the electronic media is the problem with which we are just now beginning to grapple.

Beginning with the alarming statement that over one-half of the motion pictures produced before 1951 no longer exist because of deliberate destruction, neglect, fire, and deterioration, Susan Dalton admits to the enormous challenge that lies ahead to preserve several types of moving images. Yet, there are many institutions dedicated to that effort. As she discusses problems related to the preservation of nitrate film, acetate film, cellulose triacetate-polyester film, videotape, and optical disc recording, it becomes obvious that preservation problems exist not only for the older types, but for the newer ones as well. The fact that the preserving of moving images is a difficult task requiring time, effort, and money also becomes obvious. Like the preservation of other materials, moving image preservation will require the concentrated effort of many.

After an introduction to the problems involved in newspaper preservation and a brief history of efforts to that end, Susan Garretson Swartzburg discusses the work of the United States Newspaper Project relating its preservation efforts to international attempts to preserve newspapers. She points out the need for internationally accepted policies and procedures to clarify what to preserve and how best to effect the preservation. With microfilm the currently accepted medium for newspaper preservation, Swartzburg includes a discussion of agencies involved in microfilming preservation and the techniques, procedures, standards, and specifications to be followed.

Since silver gelatin photographic films and papers have been around for a century and since by far the largest number of black-and-white photographic images are silver gelatin images, our knowledge concerning the properties of these records is extensive. Also well known are the factors which may affect their stability: relative humidity, oxidizing chemicals, temperature, light, handling, and use. The effects of these factors upon the photographs alone or in tandem are discussed, and Klaus B. Hendriks does not leave us without offering preventive measures for the preservation of photographs, including provision of correct storage conditions; use of proper storage enclosures; instructions for handling, use, and display; provision of emergency plans; and applications of copying and duplication techniques. Unfortunately, it is not possible to include here Hendrik's demonstration of one of the early processes for making a black-and-white photograph.

Every person likes to believe that his/her color photographs will last for generations just as libraries, archives, and museums hope that their collections of color photographs, including motion pictures and slides, will also endure. Henry Wilhelm's message is that many are already lost or are gradually fading and staining. He advocates humidity-controlled cold storage for long-term preservation even for cellulose nitrate films, as opposed to duplicating nitrate onto safety film as is frequently prescribed. He briefly notes the scheduled appearance of Polaroid Permanent-Color prints. These prints have images formed with special, highly stable color pigments rather than the dyes used in other types of color photographs.

Sara Wolf Green discusses the fundamental causes of the deterioration of textiles along with the techniques available for eliminating or slowing down the deterioration processes. To preserve textiles, one must possess a basic understanding of the general properties of their fibers as well as the effects of the environment on textile materials. Many of the enemies of other materials—light, temperature, humidity, pollutants—are also the enemies of textiles. Proper storage, packaging, and handling of textiles are also discussed.

Characteristics of archival records such as uniqueness, size of holdings, and the relation of individual parts to the whole, along with their complexity and diversity, have influenced the development of archival preservation programs. Mary Lynn Ritzenthaler discusses two closely related areas of preservation activities: holdings maintenance (a term devised at the United States National Archives to describe a range of basic preservation activities designed to prolong the useful life of archival records through a stable storage environment) and conservation treatment. Single item treatment and batch treatment differences are identified and documentation of treatments is discussed.

Cartographic materials come in many forms such as maps, profiles, sections, diagrams, views, globes, atlases, remote sensing imagery, plastic models, and data in digital form. The most frequent preservation problem that the map librarian or curator faces is dealing with paper preservation. Photocopying has increased the number of problems involving paper. Handling, care, and storage are other issues of map preservation which are covered by Mary Lynette Larsgaard's presentation as are those dealing with damage and repair.

Despite the many problems that have been expressed by each of the presenters, the final presenter, Carla J. Montori, remains optimistic for the future just as Lambertus van Zelst was optimistic in the first presentation. Montori is reassured by the increasing interest and activity in preservation, finding that this activity heralds institutional recognition of the issues, problems, and opportunities involved in the preservation of collections. There is widespread grappling with solutions for these problems. She finds that many problems are not yet solved, but that the initial panic is subsiding; yet there is need for a great deal of enthusiasm, commitment, and hard work (including careful planning) on the part of all who wish to participate.

Unfortunately, Mary Wood Lee's presentation on "Care of Art on Paper" is not part of the published proceedings.

Many persons are involved in the anatomy of a conference and more than can be named here should be recognized for their contributions. We are grateful to the faculty of the Graduate School of Library and Information Science (GSLIS) for choosing this topic for the 1988 conference. We acknowledge the support of Dean Leigh S. Estabrook. Annetta K. Holt of the GSLIS staff provided assistance in a myriad of ways before and during the conference. Kathryn Painter of the GSLIS staff carefully and cheerfully performed many responsibilities for the conference planners. Others of our colleagues introduced speakers.

Thomas Farrell, from Hertzberg New-Method, Inc., Jacksonville,

Illinois; Glenn Granger, from the Highsmith Company; and John Ison, from Demco, responded to our request to vendors to be a part of the informal Tuesday evening session. They presented a variety of materials to satisfy preservation needs. Carolyn Jane Gammon, Preservation/Conservation Assistant, University of Illinois at Urbana-Champaign Library, displayed tools, techniques, and materials that can be used in the local library to foster conservation activities.

In the years between 1981 to 1988, there has been increased attention to preservation in educational programs. At the GSLIS in the fall 1988 semester, the first full semester course in preservation was offered. It was a team-teaching effort of the Allerton Institute planners. The twenty students in the course were active participants in the entire conference and assisted in many ways. Their enthusiasm for and role in this conference will long be remembered.

Support in the form of a grant came from the Council on Library Resources, Inc., long a proponent for efforts featuring the preservation of library materials. Not only do we appreciate their financial backing but also the encouragement that this grant gave us.

We cannot close this introduction without commenting once again on the participants and the presenters. One of our colleagues remarked that he considers a conference a success when every seat is filled for every session. He commented that by that criterion this was a successful conference. To each of the speakers who held the attention of the participants, we are grateful; and to those who attended and listened and to those who will read the proceedings and carry out suggestions that came from the conference, we are equally grateful.

WILLIAM T HENDERSON
KATHRYN LUTHER HENDERSON
Editors

LAMBERTUS VAN ZELST

Director
Conservation Analytical Laboratory
Smithsonian Institution
Washington, D.C.

Needs and Potential Solutions in Conservation

INTRODUCTION

There is a certain challenge to discussing the conservation needs of nonbook materials at a meeting of library specialists. While most of the presentations in this volume deal with the preservation of nonbook materials which librarians may very well encounter in the collections of their institutions, this paper addresses the "state of conservation" in general, in or outside the library field. To do so, the author did not have to start from scratch; in fact, his homework had been done already by the National Institute for Conservation of Cultural Property (NIC), about which more will be said later in this paper.

This paper uses as its reference point Figure 1. This figure, prepared by NIC, gives an overall assessment of the existing needs in various areas. The intensity of the shading represents the urgency of the need to address any individual activity. As one sees immediately, the library and fine arts fields are relatively the best off, with natural history collections in the worst overall state. This figure compares the relative condition of each specialty field within each activity.

Public Awareness

The first column in Figure 1 deals with the degree of public awareness. One hardly needs to emphasize the importance of this educational endeavor; without a broad-based public understanding and support of the conservation and preservation needs of the nation's cultural property, these activities will not be assigned the relatively high priority on the list of civic responsibilities necessary to obtain and sustain

AN ASSESSMENT OF THE CURRENT STATE OF ACTIVITIES REQUIRED FOR
THE CONTINUING CARE OF OUR NATIONAL PATRIMONY
Prepared by the National Institute for the Conservation of Cultural Property

Draft - March 23, 1990 © NIC	Public Awareness	Professional Information		Professional Training			Research		Preventive Care and Treatment
		Conservators	Other Professionals, e.g., curators & architects	Conservators	Other Professionals, e.g., curators & architects		Basic & Applied	Analytical Services	
Historic Preservation The built environment: the American contribution.									
Anthropology (Archeology & Ethnography) Material evidences of past & present cultures.									
Archives & Libraries Documents recording the human experience and aspirations.									
Fine Arts Artistic works that embody human creativity.									
History Historical objects illuminating the American past.									
Natural History The natural world and how we relate to it.									

Figure 1. The lighter the shade the better this activity is being addressed. For example, the area that is most adequately addressed is the training of conservators of fine arts. However, even in this area much remains to be done. There is a need to strengthen the existing training programs financially so they have adequate ongoing operating support.

the needed public and private funding. The field of Architectural and Historic Preservation has done the best job so far; one needs only to think about the relatively large number of members of the National Trust for Historic Preservation who receive *Historic Preservation*, and the existence of a federally chartered and funded Advisory Council for Historic Preservation, which plays a significant role in the formulation of federal government policies regarding historic preservation issues. Archives, libraries, and fine arts museums still have a lot to do. The archives and library fields, especially, have more recently made significant progress in this regard through "brittle book" campaigns such as the *Slow Fires* videotape and the successful subsequent call for Congressional funding through the National Endowment for the Humanities. History, natural history, and anthropology collections are by far the worst off because there is very little public awareness of their conservation and preservation needs. Certainly, part of the reason for this shortfall lies in the fact that these collections, especially those in anthropology and natural history, are of a systematic type and exist primarily for research purposes. Consequently, one is dealing with extremely large collections, generally orders of magnitude larger that fine arts collections, and only a minor fraction of these collections is on public view, while the major part remains in storage. As a result, the public has very little concept of the extent of the preservation problem in these collections. An additional difficulty comes in bringing the point across that, for example, even rock specimens in mineralogy collections do deteriorate under inappropriate conditions and need preservation care. History collections often share the same problem of disproportion between collection size and the number of items on public view. Moreover, many of these collections are housed in relatively small institutions—historic houses, small local museums—and hence do not have the visibility which display in a large institution affords. This, of course, also affects those systematic collections housed in university museums, a significant fraction of natural history and anthropology collections.

Both NIC and the American Institute for Conservation of Historic and Artistic Works (AIC)—the professional organization for conservators and other conservation professionals—have earmarked raising public awareness as a high priority. One problem lies in the funding, as this has to be sought in the private sector, and public awareness campaigns can be quite costly. The successes in the architectural preservation field provide good examples of mechanisms which can be employed profitably. The campaign around the restoration of the Statue of Liberty shows the benefit of tying in with a "spectacular" project. Even controversies can be used to advantage: the recent discussions around the cleaning of the Sistine Chapel frescoes have certainly brought some of the issues in conservation to the attention of a wider audience. The National Trust's success was already referred to above; one might speculate that a magazine similar to *Historic Preservation* but devoted to the preservation and conservation of the other components of the nation's cultural patrimony should be equally attractive to the public.

Professional Information

The second column in Figure 1, Professional Information, is split into two subheadings: Conservators and Other Professionals. The first subcolumn deals with the amount of technical information available to conservation professionals and the ease with which they can obtain this information. While there is a certain amount of variability, the situation here is not too bad, with the notable exception of natural history collections. The professional organizations, such as the American Institute for Conservation of Historic and Artistic Works (AIC), the International Institute for Conservation of Historic and Artistic Works (IIC), and the Association for Preservation Technology (APT), to mention a few of the most prominent ones, publish technical journals and organize regular technical meetings which allow for a constant flow of information. It is worthwhile noting that conservators working in fine arts, anthropology, history, and archival and library collections deal with the same basic materials and thus can share to a large extent the same technical information. This holds to a lesser extent, of course, once preservation issues come in because now the nature of the collection, its use and size, come to play a differentiating role. The situation in natural history specimen conservation, although still rather bleak, can look forward to improvements in the not-too-distant future with the establishment of a professional organization in this field, the Society for Preservation of Natural History Collections (SPNHC). The Society publishes a biennial journal. The dissemination of technical information through the journals and meetings of the professional organizations is typically financed from membership dues, subscriptions, and registration fees. Other technical conferences and symposia are regularly organized with financial assistance from foundations and the private sector.

A rather recent initiative, which greatly increases the ease and speed with which conservators can have access to the existing body of technical information, is the international Conservation Information Network (CIN). This computer network pools the information resources of the conservation community. Financial assistance has come from the Getty Conservation Institute and the active collaboration of that institution, the Canadian Conservation Institute (CCI), the Smithsonian's Conservation Analytical Laboratory (CAL), the International Centre for the Study of the Preservation and the Restoration of Cultural Property (ICCROM) in Rome, the International Council of Museums (ICOM) in Paris, and the International Council on Monuments and Sites (ICOMOS), also in Paris. Through CIN, professionals in many countries can have online access to large bibliographic and material databases housed in the computers of the Canadian Heritage Information Network (CHIN). Discussions are ongoing with the Library of Congress on the addition of a comprehensive book conservation and preservation component.

Less rose-colored is the situation with regard to the provision of professional conservation information to other nonconservation professionals such as curators, architects, librarians, archivists, registrars, etc. It seems that the way to deal with this situation is to build bridges between the professional organizations of conservators (AIC, APT, etc.) and those of other professionals such as the American Association of Museums (AAM), the Association of Systematic Collections (ASC); the American Institute of Architects (AIA); the three major organizations of American archaeologists: Archaeological Institute of America (AIA), Society for American Archaeology (SAA) and the American Anthropological Association (AAA); the American Library Association (ALA); the Society of American Archivists (SAA); and a number of others. AIC, for one, is presently taking steps to open up more interactive relationships with a number of these organizations. Organizing special sessions at annual meetings could be an especially effective way of distributing the information.

Professional Training

The third column in Figure 1, Professional Training, again is split between training for conservation professionals and conservation training for other professionals. The brightest spot on the chart refers to the professional training for conservators in fine arts collections. This is to a large extent the consequence of the history of conservation, which saw its origins in the arts conservation field. Presently, there are three academic training programs for conservators catering to the fine arts field, although graduates from these programs also find frequent employment in archaeology and ethnography museums, history museums, and libraries or archives. These programs are operated by the University of Delaware, New York University, and the State University College at Buffalo, New York. Each program confers a Master's degree in Arts or Science, and, depending on the program, a certificate in conservation. Typically, students are trained at the graduate level over a period of three or four years to become experts in such specialties as the conservation of paintings, works of art on paper, textiles, three-dimensional objects, furniture, etc. The students spend one year in practical training as interns with an established conservator. Each of the programs graduates an average of ten conservators annually. The library and archives field draws to some extent on the paper conservators trained in the programs referred to above, but also has a special conservation training program at Columbia University. The latter school additionally operates a small training program in architectural conservation. The demand for architectural preservation specialists, however, is not met through American training programs. Many American architects have attended the programs offered by ICCROM in Rome (more about this organization will be discussed later in this paper) or in York, England. Several American universities offer programs in historic preservation, but they tend to be less technical in nature.

History museums are to a certain extent served by the flow of objects conservators coming out of the training programs. However, the conservation of technology history collections (for example, historic machinery, airplanes, trains, and automobiles) entails a large number of issues, both philosophical and practical, which are totally different from the more traditional conservation of three-dimensional arts museum objects. Presently, no programs dedicate courses to these specialties, and technology museums must depend on a blend of conventionally trained objects conservators with technological specialists trained within the crafts tradition (for example, airplane maintenance mechanics). Similarly, archaeology and ethnography collections depend to a large extent on the objects conservators who graduate from the training programs, but again, a great need exists for specially trained conservators for such collections and for work on excavation sites. Some American conservators have been trained at institutions in England and Canada, but a study by the National Institute for Conservation has established that the need is large enough to justify a national training program in archaeologic and ethnographic conservation.

Academic conservation programs depend heavily on outside funding, especially for tuition and student stipend support. Both government funding, through the National Endowments of the Arts and Humanities and the National Museum Act, and private funding, especially from a number of foundations such as the Mellon, Kress, and Getty Foundations, have been of critical importance in this respect. Unfortunately, the termination of the National Museum Act and reduced funding by other federal agencies, which cannot be compensated for with foundation support, have resulted in serious financial problems for these programs.

It should be emphasized that academic graduate programs are by no means the only way to train conservators. In the art conservation as well as the book conservation field, apprenticeship training has been a time-honored method of education. A well-designed and personalized apprenticeship can be at least as fruitful as academic training and may often offer additional benefits in that much more attention can be given to the development of hands-on skills. However, when addressing the national need for skilled professionals, the efficiency of the academic programs in training relatively large numbers of students simultaneously offers a clear advantage. A new and rather innovative training mechanism was adopted by the Smithsonian Institution's Conservation Analytical Laboratory (CAL) for its Furniture Conservation Training Program. Because the traditional training programs could not fill the need for furniture specialists by far, a different approach was sought. As a result, experienced wood craftspeople, who do not need training in construction methods and other woodcrafts skills, are trained in the necessary conservation skills through a program which combines twelve two-week courses taught at CAL with a regime of intensive home study. This allows the students to maintain regular employment while following the three-year study program. A fourth year is spent again in practical internships with established furniture conservators. Through a collaborative agreement with Adelphi (Ohio) University, it is possible for students in this program to obtain a Master's degree with the completion of their study, in addition to the Smithsonian's certificate. This program is financed entirely by CAL, although the students are expected to take care of their own travel and lodging expenses connected with course attendance.

It was already mentioned that the academic training involves one year of internship spent with an established conservator. Generally, it is agreed that additional internship training after completion of the academic program is not only highly beneficial but almost essential because it provides the recently graduated conservator with "hands-on" experience in a "real life" situation. A number of such internship opportunities are available at a variety of institutions. Funding for these internships is made available by a number of foundations and institutions. Practicing conservators still have the need for advanced courses in specialized subjects and periodical refresher courses. These are organized by the professional organizations, as well as by a number of institutions, among which the Getty Conservation Institute and CAL are especially active.

Conservation Training for Other Professionals

In regard to the subject of the second subcolumn in Figure 1, Conservation Training for Other Professionals, the state of affairs provides less reason for exuberance. Figure 1 shows that the darkest area of shading pertains to the areas of anthropology and natural history.

Indeed, anthropologists, biologists, and mineralogists, to name some of the professionals most frequently found to be charged with the curation of such collections, generally will receive no training related to preservation issues whatsoever in their professional education. In fact, one major problem, especially in natural history collections, is that the typical curator of such collections has received no museology training at all. The situation is hardly much better in history collections and in architecture. The most enlightened professionals seem to reside in fine arts museums, libraries, and archives. However, there is no reason yet to rest on unearned laurels; many of the academic museology programs do not have a significant conservation component, and fine arts curators often enter the profession through a different path, i.e., graduate studies in art history. Clearly, raising awareness through professional organizations is much needed. If such organizations, in collaboration with conservation organizations such as AIC, could convince the academic departments involved to add appropriate conservation components to their course package, very significant progress could result. Some of these professional organizations are presently considering the possibility of establishing an accreditation system for training programs. Certainly, the conservation community would be delighted to play an advisory role in determining minimum standards for the contents of appropriate conservation courses.

Research

The next column heading in Figure 1 is somewhat of a misnomer: it really should be called Scientific Support. The subheadings are then Research and Analytical Services. The first subcolumn, Research, deals with the amount of research in conservation science and technology done for various types of collections. To elucidate these terms, *conservation science* concerns itself with the understanding and characterization of the processes, chemical and physical, which play a role in the deterioration of objects and the materials from which they are composed, and with evaluating the factors which influence the rates at which these processes take place. Such information can lead to the formulation of optimum conditions for storage, exhibiting, transit, etc. and form the basis, too, for conservation technology research. The latter type of research, *technology* endeavors to develop and test treatment techniques for objects in unstable conditions. Both types of research are closely interrelated and should preferably not be pursued in isolation. Also, the research teams ideally should be comprised of both conservators and physical scientists.

The Research column in Figure 1 shows a quite stark contrast between the fields for fine arts, libraries and archives, which appear relatively light, and the other types of collections. Again, this is largely due to historic developments. Much of the early work was done within the conservation departments of the larger art museums and major libraries and archives. These large institutions recognized the need for research in preservation issues affecting their collections. Realizing that their interests were at stake, they took the necessary steps either to initiate this research in-house or to sponsor it through outside research establishments. This is not meant at all to negate the very significant contributions made, especially in the area of treatment technology, by dedicated individual conservators, including private practitioners. They, however, also came from the fields of fine arts and libraries. More recently, a shift seems to be occurring, due to the establishment of a few major research laboratories dedicated to the improvement of collections care. Some of these, such as the Canadian Conservation Institute (CCI), the Getty Conservation Institute (GCI) and the Smithsonian's Conservation Analytical Laboratory (CAL), are rather eclectic in their choice of research programs and may cover a wide range; others, such as the laboratories of the Library of Congress and the National Archives, are principally dedicated to work pertaining to the collection which they serve. Of course, the results obtained in the latter type of laboratories are equally important to the preservation of collections in other libraries and archives. As with all scientific research, this type of work can be extremely expensive. While support for conservation research can be obtained from several funding agencies and foundations, the amounts of individual grants are generally such that only limited projects can be undertaken. As a result, larger, specialized laboratories play a more significant role because they have the necessary equipment and staff resources provided for in their regular budgets and can run a number of projects simultaneously.

From the shading of the other fields in the Research column in Figure 1, it is clear that these fields are quite far behind in the development of research data that support the conservation and preservation of their collections. However, the shift referred to in the preceding paragraph may well be of help here. The new, large laboratories may be able to address some of the research needs of these fields, allocating resources on a scale which will allow for greater efficiency than otherwise obtainable. As an example, even in the darkest area—the natural history collections—some recent research initiatives by laboratories at Carnegie-Mellon and CAL may be expected to result in the production of some highly needed data. In natural history collections, especially, an immense amount of work is necessary. Recent developments in scientific research technology, especially in the biological sciences, and the resulting new uses of the research collections as, for example, in the DNA characterization to establish philogenetic relationships, have placed completely new restrictions on the actual intervention allowable in conservation and preservation treatments of specimens in such collections. Preservation of modern synthetic materials is another area in which research is greatly needed. While data from such research will be of great utility in fields such as fine arts collections, especially those involving contemporary art works, the greatest impact would be in the technology and history collections, where objects composed of these materials enter the collections in enormous numbers and presently pose often insolvable preservation problems. Again, the attention of the research institutions must be directed to these problems, and some of the new initiatives indicate that this is happening. A major problem is posed, though, by the shortage of conservation scientists, i.e. physical scientists with a specialization in this type of research. A recently initiated graduate training program operated collaboratively by the Johns Hopkins University and the Smithsonian's Conservation Analytical Laboratory, which leads to a PhD in materials science with a subspecialty in conservation science, is a first attempt at formulating a remedy for this longstanding problem.

Analytical Services

Analytical support for conservation practitioners is a different matter. Conservators engaged in the care of collections and the treatment of instable objects regularly have an urgent need for analytical assistance. Sometimes the questions are of a relatively straightforward nature, requiring rather routine analytical techniques, but on other occasions complicated processes must be evaluated, or analyses are needed which require the use of very sophisticated analytical technology and specialized expertise. A complicating factor is that objects have typically quite unique problems because of their individual composition and history. Hence, there is a need for customized analytical services in that the scientist who will perform the work must be fully informed and understanding of the particular problem and object for which the analysis is required. Thus, the scientist must collaborate closely with the conservator to ensure that the proper analytical techniques will be used and appropriate samples selected if necessary. This requirement makes it very difficult to use, for example, commercial analytical laboratories: when the conservator takes samples in isolation from the analyst and then mails them to the latter, chances are all too great that the answers obtained will be rather meaningless in the context of the real question at hand. This situation also makes the usefulness of a central laboratory to serve a national or large regional area highly questionable.

A look at the column for Analytical Services in Figure 1 clarifies immediately that this is one of the bleakest areas in regard to unserviced needs. One of the major problems is cost. Setting up a basic support laboratory for a typical museum will require an initial investment of the order of one million dollars; also, the operating costs are quite high, as equipment needs to be capitalized and maintained, while the salary costs for scientific staff are more than museums are accustomed to. A few of the major museums, libraries and archives, recognizing the constant need for analytical support, have been able to afford these expenses, but for many medium-size and smaller institutions, the cost is too high. This leaves the conservators in such institutions, as well as those in private practice, with the problem of where to get the help they need. For many of the more simple analytical needs, where a material needs to be identified with routine techniques, local university or even industrial laboratories may well be of assistance, provided, again, that the question to which the analysis should provide an answer is thoroughly discussed with the collaborating scientist. Indeed, many conservators have established good personal relationships with scientists in such local institutions and make regular use of this acquaintance. However, in the frequent cases where the problem is more complicated and the scientist has to have a certain background in conservation issues, most conservators have a very hard time finding help. Various mechanisms have been suggested to alleviate this problem. Most prominent among these has figured the notion of a large central service laboratory which would serve the nation. However, because of the impossibility to maintain the direct collaborative relation between the conservator requesting the assistance and the scientist who will do the analytical work, this idea does not seem to offer a feasible solution. Certainly, large central laboratories could play a useful role in doing research in conservation science and technology, and as mentioned before, this is actually happening. The analytical support, however, needs to be administered on a more local level. Present thinking tends to point in the direction of regional laboratories, with each covering an area whose size allows the scientists to go to the collections served, or the conservators with their objects to come to the laboratory. An analog here exists already for the provision of actual conservation services in the so-called regional laboratories, which will be discussed later. One could visualize regional analytical centers set up along the same lines, or even using the existing regional conservation centers and operated under cooperative agreements between regional institutions and private conservators. Another variation foresees the establishment of a national institute, not housed in a large central laboratory, but consisting of a series of regional subsidiaries. A recently initiated action group, the Center for Advancement of Preservation Technology (CAPT), which has its roots in the archaeological community, proposes to establish a network of such regional centers within cooperating universities. At present, however, conservators have to use the help where they can find it. Luckily, a number of the institutional laboratories will take on outside work from colleagues in other institutions or private practice. A recent study conducted, but not yet published, under the aegis of AIC, has surveyed the institutions which are able and willing to share such resources. It is important to note again, though, that scientific support is relatively expensive, and conservation budgets need to allow for these costs.

Preventive Care and Treatment

The last column of Figure 1 is Preventive Care and Treatment. Here can be seen how much actual care collections of various types receive. This picture emerges: the situation is relatively the best in fine arts museums, followed by libraries and archives and architectural and historic preservation, and rather bleak in other areas, especially in natural history and archaeology collections. Also, it is very clear that even in those "enlightened" areas there is more than enough room for improvement. This situation has arisen from a combination of reasons. A general malaise results from the cost associated with these activities which definitely affects the operating budget of the institution housing the collections. This, in combination with the lack of awareness of the imperative for conservation, has often led to a too-low position of conservation in the institutional priorities. That art museums historically have been leaders in the provision of conservation care to their collections certainly is due in part to the fact that the monetary value of the collections provides an incentive. Most large-size and many medium-size museums today have inhouse conservation departments, as do a number of major libraries and archives. Over the last fifteen years, a number of so-called regional laboratories have been established; these serve a number of institutions in their geographic area which could not afford individual inhouse laboratories. Often, they are organized as consortia of these institutions. Several such regional centers specialize in servicing libraries and archives. Finally, the increased awareness of the need for conservation care, combined with improved funding possibilities for conservation operation expenses through the National Endowments and, especially, the Institute for Museum Services (IMS), have led to a significantly increased demand for services of conservators in private practice. As a result, the number of such independently operating conservators has seen a corresponding rise. To help institutions in finding conservators who will accept private practice work, AIC has established a referral system which classifies conservators by specialty and geographic location.

Summary of Figure 1

As discussed earlier, enhanced public awareness of the need for historic preservation is certainly an important factor in the status of care given to architectural preservation, as is the financial rewards incentive. The situation in anthropology and natural history collections is by far the worst. Most recently, awareness of the conservation needs for these collections has started to rise among the curators and other professionals in charge of such collections. As they also are eligible for some of the funding for conservation care, one might expect the situation in these collections to show some improvement in the future. The difficulties, on the other hand, are many: the size of the collections, enormous by fine arts collection standards, and the already-mentioned lack of research data and of specialized conservators. These factors, as well as the need to minimize intervention which is dictated by the research use of these collections, result in an emphasis on prevention rather than remedial treatment. The trend towards prevention has become prevalent in other museums: the improvement of storage and exhibit environments results in a larger benefit to more objects than a concentration on individual treatments after objects have become the victim of improper environments. Of course, factors other than environment can also necessitate conservation treatment, but too often in the past, objects were returned from the conservation laboratory to the same conditions which had caused their instability in the first place. IMS, a major funding source for conservation assistance, has established priorities for funding in which collection surveys top the list, followed by modifications to the physical plant for improvement of storage and exhibit environment, all before actual treatments of individual objects.

PROFESSIONAL ORGANIZATIONS

It might be of interest now to look at some of the organizations which play major roles in this field. Already mentioned several times was NIC, the National Institute for Conservation of Cultural Property. NIC is a national organization which provides a forum and clearinghouse for institutions and organizations with an interest in conservation, either as users or providers. One of its major functions is to assess needs in conservation and formulate national strategies to address those needs. Both under its former identity as the National Conservation Advisory

Council (NCAC) and its present structure, it has conducted comprehensive studies of needs in particular areas of conservation, which have been published in a series of special reports. Coordination of projects to address the identified needs is performed, identifying appropriate organizations and institutions to run these projects, bringing them together and assisting in finding the necessary funding. Its role in raising public awareness of conservation has been mentioned already.

AIC is primarily an organization of individual conservation professionals, although others can be nonprofessional members; a special category exists for institutional members. Its goals are overall educational, providing mechanisms for exchange of professional information within the conservation community, raising and maintaining professional standards, and promoting the state of conservation through educational outreach to related professions as well as the general public. AIC's Code of Ethics and Standards of Practice provide professional standards and rules of conduct with which professional AIC members are bound to comply. AIC publishes the scholarly *Journal of the American Institute for Conservation*, which contains technical and scientific articles of interest to the conservation professional, and a bimonthly newsletter. The Annual Meeting provides members with the opportunity to present papers of a technical nature for discussion with their peers. Within AIC, a number of so-called Specialty Groups have been organized, which provide members with a forum to discuss technical and other issues of specific relevance to a particular conservation specialization. These groups organize individual technical sessions at the Annual Meeting, and several produce specialized technical publications. Of special interest to the readers of this paper may be the Book and Paper Group of AIC, which among others has published its *Book and Paper Annual* since 1982. AIC's educational goals and activities are also pursued and supported by the Foundation of the American Institute for the Conservation of Historic and Artistic Works (FAIC). FAIC operates several endowments that support the attendance of students at professional meetings and provide assistance for the production of technical publications, the organization of small symposia and refresher courses, and the individual pursuit of projects aimed at professional advancement. One of the Endowment funds, established in honor of well-known book conservator Carolyn Horton, specifically provides support to students in book conservation.

Professionals engaged in architectural conservation and historic preservation in the United States and Canada are likely to maintain membership in the Association for Preservation Technology (APT). This organization publishes the *APT Bulletin: The Journal of Preservation Technology* and *Communique*, and organizes annual technical meetings. Many American conservators also maintain membership in one of several international professional organizations. Most are members of the International Institute for Conservation of Historic and Artistic Works (IIC). This organization, based in London, also has chapters in a large number of countries. In fact, AIC originally was the American Group of IIC, but became an independent organization partially for legal reasons. IIC publishes the journal *Studies in Conservation*, a *Bulletin* and, until recently, the *Art and Archaeology Technical Abstracts* (AATA). Now *AATA* is published by the Getty Conservation Institute in association with IIC. In addition to the printed version, this journal is now also accessible online through the Conservation Information Network (CIN). IIC organizes a biennial international conference where conservators from many countries present technical papers which are published in the *Preprints*. Another major international organization is the Conservation Committee of ICOM, the International Council of Museums. ICOM's Conservation Committee is organized in technical work groups which meet during the triennial meeting of the Conservation Committee. The Committee publishes elaborate *Preprints* of papers presented at the meeting.

A very important organization is the International Centre for the Study of the Preservation and Restoration of Cultural Property (IC-CROM). This organization, based in Rome, is organized along the same lines as UNESCO, i.e., with membership of countries, including the United States, who pay an annual contribution which is based on their UNESCO assessment. ICCROM plays a major international educational role. It provides courses, both short and long, in areas where little training is available elsewhere. These include specialties for which little or no training opportunities exist in the United States. Thus for a long time ICCROM was the only place where architects could receive training in architectural conservation. Other examples of such courses are the mural painting course, and a course on the scientific principles in conservation. A major activity of ICCROM is its assistance to developing countries in the preservation of their cultural property. ICCROM will organize technical missions to such countries in order to provide actual assistance while training local staff. The PREMA course is a new training program in preventive collection care, especially designed for African countries. ICCROM also is a major international information center. It maintains a very large technical library and a bibliographic abstract database, which is accessible through the Conservation Information Network. Its publication program produces a number of specialized books annually, as well as international indices on conservation training programs and ongoing conservation research.

CONCLUSION

Conservation is a field in motion, with great needs and difficulties, but also with active progress and great promises. Conservation in the United States, as well as worldwide, has enormous challenges to meet, but it has come a long way and should be able to maintain its progress. On a wall of the American Institute for Conservation of Historic and Artistic Works hangs a framed quotation, attributed to Goethe, that transcends both time and place:

> Works of art are the property of mankind and ownership carries with it the obligation to preserve them. He who neglects this duty and directly or indirectly contributes to their damage or ruin invites the reproach of barbarism and will be punished with the contempt of all educated people, now and in future ages.

This directive, applied to all cultural property which citizens of the world own collectively, is still and even more valid today. Conservators have their task cut out for them and cannot afford to fail.

DENNIS INCH

Vice-President
Light Impressions, Inc.
Rochester, New York

The Role of Vendors in Conservation

This discussion will advise in four areas of conservation:

1. What are the responsibilities of an archival supplier?
2. What is the range of supplies needed to care for a photographic collection?
3. How does one company (Light Impressions) stay current in the changing field of photographic preservation?
4. What are some of the problems encountered in a storage environment?

Responsibilities

The most important responsibility of the archival supplier is to test products before introducing them to the marketplace. This should be in two phases: Is the material safe for the intended purpose, and is the design correct?

The second most important responsibility of the archival supplier is to control the quality of the raw materials to ensure that specifications are met. This applies to paper, plastic, adhesives—whatever the products are made of.

A third responsibility of the supplier is to stand behind the products with a return policy for replacement or complete credit if or when problems arise.

Fourth, the supplier is responsible for providing complete descriptions and specifications on products and their intended uses.

Supplies

Supplies needed to care for a photographic collection are outlined in the following chart.

Prints	
STORAGE & PRESENTATION **matted & unmatted prints,** **photographs, fine art prints,** **newspapers, collectibles, ephemera,** **maps**	Portfolio Boxes Manuscript Boxes Museum Cases Drop-Front Boxes Flat Storage Boxes Steel Flat Files
TRANSPORTATION OF MATTED **& UNMATTED PRINTS**	Print Shipping Cases
ENCLOSURES FOR MATTED & **UNMATTED PRINTS**	Flap Storage Envelopes Fold Lock Sleeves Thumb-Cut Envelopes Handling Folders Map Folders Polyethylene Bags Polyester Film for Encapsulation Interleaving Papers Renaissance Paper (nonbuffered) Apollo Paper (buffered) Neutral Glassine (buffered)
MATTING FOR PRINTS	Exeter Conservation Board Nonbuffered Rag Board Westminster 100% Rag Board
PRINT HINGING, MUSEUM **MOUNTING, PHOTO CORNERS,** **MOUNTING ADHESIVES**	Linen Tape (acid-free) Mounting Corners (clear) Paper Photo Corners (acid-free) Paper Tape (acid-free) Hinging Paper Methyl Cellulose Rice Starch Thymol Wheat Starch
DRY MOUNTING & WET **MOUNTING ADHESIVES**	Dry Mounting Tissue PVA Glue Elvace 40704 Positionable Mounting Adhesive
DRY MOUNTING EQUIPMENT	Dry Mounting Presses Tacking Iron Flat Plate
Conservation	
ENCAPSULATION	Mylar "Type D" Film Double-Coated Film Tape #415 Table Top Cornerounder Gloves
DEACIDIFICATION	Wei T'o Solutions
pH TESTING	pH Testing Pen
TEMPERATURE & HUMIDITY **INDICATORS**	Desiccant Canisters Recording Thermometer/Hygrometer Humidity Indicator Hygrometer RH Indicator Cards

Figure 1. Product Reference Chart (*cont.*)

Conservation (*continued*)	
SPECIALTY PAPERS	Blotting Paper
	Wrapping Paper
	Archival Corrugated Board
	Interleaving Tissue (buffered & non-buffered)
	Neutral Glassine
Collections	
ALBUMS, SCRAPBOOKS	Archival Scrapbooks
	Archival Albums
ALBUM PAGES **photographs** **post cards** **ephemera collections**	PhotoGuard Pages Top Loaders Mylar Sheet Protectors Acid-Free Replacement Pages
STEREOCARD & POSTCARD STORAGE & DISPLAY	Stereocard Storage Kit Postcard Storage Kit Polyethylene Bags Fold Lock Sleeves PhotoGuard Pages CardFile Boxes
DOCUMENT STORAGE & FILING	FlipTop Document Boxes File Folder (acid-free) Document Storage Kit Open Document Files Records Storage Box
Negatives & Transparencies	
NEGATIVE STORAGE	NegaGuard Systems for 35mm, 120 Film, 4x5, 5x7, & 8x10 Negative File Folders Fold Lock Sleeves Interleaving Folders Thumb-Cut Envelopes (buffered & nonbuffered) Polyethylene Thumb-Cut Envelopes Flap Envelopes Seamless Envelopes Straight Cut Envelopes Glass Plate Folders Flip Top Boxes Vapor Seal Envelopes
SLIDE STORAGE **pages, boxes, cabinets**	SlideGuard Pages TransView Sleeves Slide Cabinets Slide Storage Boxes
MAGNIFIERS	Standing Magnifier Peak 8X Loupe
PENS & INKS	Archival Inks Film & Print Marking Pens

Figure 1 (*cont.*). Product Reference Chart

How One Company Keeps Current

Staying current with changing standards in photographic conservation is a responsibility that Light Impressions lives up to on a continuing basis. Participation in the American National Standards Institute (ANSI) Committee IT9 on Permanence and Physical Properties of Imaging Media is an important part of this effort. Other organizational memberships are held in TAPPI and the American Institute for the Conservation of Historic and Artistic Works (AIC). Company representatives attend seminars and symposia on a wide variety of conservation topics from paper preservation to photography. Light Impressions is also a member of the Board of Directors of the Image Permanence Institute and the Visual Studies Workshop.

Problems in a Storage Environment

Some of the most common problems concerning the storage environment have not changed much throughout the history of photography. The first area of concern is the stability of photographic prints and negatives. If there are unstable materials such as nitrate film, these should not be integrated with the rest of the collection but stored separately using proper procedures for this type of medium. Second, adhesives, matboards, papers, and storage enclosures can be a source of deterioration. Adhesives can support a healthy community of mold which is decidedly unhealthy for the prints. Contemporary adhesives can also cause problems—e.g., magnetic pages in photo albums can cause marks to appear on the backs of the prints. More commonly, the adhesive loses its ability to hold the prints in place, causing them to fall off the page. Failure to use matboard in a frame can cause moisture to adhere the photographic print to the glass. If a matboard of low quality paper is used, acidity and other impurities such as lignin will affect the photograph. Regarding the care of envelopes and album pages, one should make sure the material meets the highest standards, since envelopes and album pages are in direct contact with the image. Thus, both high-quality materials must be used and archival procedures followed to provide a stable environment for photographic collections.

GERALD D. GIBSON

Head, Curatorial Section
Motion Picture, Broadcasting, and Recorded Sound Division
Library of Congress
Washington, D. C.

Preservation and Conservation of Sound Recordings

INTRODUCTION

On the basis of directly related scientific study, comparatively little is known about the preservation, conservation, aging problems, or properties of sound recordings. With the exception of work now being carried out on magnetic tape for the National Archives by the National Bureau of Standards (United States, 1986) and of research by the Ministere de la Culture et de la Communication for the Bibliotheque Nationale (Fontaine, 1987) on the effects of fire upon sound and audiovisual recording, virtually no independent work is going on in these areas. Most of what is known, and the basis for much of conservation practice, is carried over from other fields of research. Prior to completion of the two studies mentioned above, the primary independent document in this field has been *Preservation and Storage of Sound Recordings* (Pickett & Lemcoe, 1959).

The Pickett and Lemcoe study, though out of print, is still valid today and is the basis of most of the conservation work in the field. Yet several topics are excluded in their report; for example, cylinders, laser discs, some of the more unusual disc formats, and digital recordings. Tape recordings are covered only briefly. Thus the majority of recommendations presented today are based upon daily trial-and-error. Further work comparable to that carried out by Pickett and Lemcoe, and the ARSC/AAA's NEH-funded study entitled *Audio Preservation: A Planning Study* as well as those now underway at the National Bureau of Standards and the Ministere de la Culture et de la Communication are greatly needed.

This article's coverage of the various sound carriers which have

27

been produced over the years is limited to those most frequently encountered in the modern working collection or in most archives, i.e., cylinder, disc, and tape recordings.

MATERIALS USED IN SOUND RECORDINGS

The initial problem that one encounters in attempting to conserve and preserve sound recordings is recognizing the various materials of which they are made. For example, in successfully cleaning a recording, one of the essential acts in conserving the medium, is based in large part on recognizing the type of recording (i.e., CD or disc) and its component materials. It is essential to know that a CD is safely cleaned by wiping it in a spoke fashion from the center, i.e., across the grooves, while other discs must be cleaned by wiping in a circular or spiral direction and not across the grooves. It is equally important to know that various chemicals which may be helpful in safely cleaning a vinyl disc will destroy shellac. Similar problems exist in the cleaning of all other audio formats as well.

Ever since the disc was first introduced by Emile Berliner in 1887, many forms of the disc have been and are still widely available: LPs, 45s, 78s, acetates, and CDs. These forms are all so well-standardized that they lead the modern librarian/archivist to assume that such was always the case. However, the disc has evolved through many phases, each reflecting the specific needs or proclivities of a given inventor, manufacturer, or patent holder. Innovations have included such techniques as hill-and-dale recording, inside-out tracking, and laterally and vertically cut grooves. Some manufacturers have done such things as putting two spindles on a turntable so that the owner of the machine would have to buy records which would accommodate such a double spindle system. Disc recordings may vary in size from approximately 1 inch to 23 inches or more in diameter, and from 1/64th inch or less to 1/4 inch or more in thickness. They have been made of many substances, from wax and wood pulp to exotic, rare, and costly metals. They can be very stable and chemically inert, highly combustible and corrosive, or anywhere in between.

The signal on a disc may be analog or digital, recorded acoustically, electrically or optically, using either a lateral or a vertical cutting head and playback stylus or a laser, and produced by several processes—cutting, embossing, magnetizing, and photographic engraving. The recording so produced may be a totally unique item which never leaves the confines of the area in which it is made, or it may be part of a commercial mass production with worldwide distribution. Discs can play at speeds of less than ten to greater than 500 revolutions per minute (RPM). Their styli — when they use one — may have a tip radius varying from .5 to 35 mils, with intended tracking weights of less than .25 gram to several pounds or more.

LPs and 45s are generally made of various plastics and plastic compounds. CDs are laminates of plastics and various metal foils, with sundry lacquers used to seal the package. The archival collection, and even the library collection in some notable cases, will add 78s and acetate discs to this "most common disc formats" list. The 78s were generally made of shellac and shellac compounds, though there were a notable number made of plastics, rubber, cellulose, and various laminate combinations. Acetate discs are laminates with a base of metal, wood products or glass, with a coating of either ethyl cellulose, cellulose acetate, or nitrocellulose.

Cylinders come in sizes almost as varied as those cited for discs, ranging in diameter from 1 5/16 inches (Bell & Tainter) through 5 inches (concert size) to the much larger pantograph masters used by such firms as Pathe. Lengths vary from half an inch (talking doll) through 8 inches (dictaphone) and more. The recordings were limited to hill-and-dale and mono, although the number of grooves per inch varied from 100 to 200.

The most common-sized cylinders are 2.1875 inches by 4.25 inches, generally made of various celluloid compounds. However, wax cylinders were made in the hundreds of thousands, and it is not unusual to find them today. As a matter of fact, the Library of Congress has just received its first cylinder on copyright deposit this past year!

Celluloid cylinders are made of nitrocellulose with an additive of camphor. Though well-known in some circles, this fact seems to have escaped most, if not all, sound archivists and collectors. Nitrocellulose is quite flammable and, if in an advanced stage of deterioration, is potentially hazardous. This fact was called to the attention of the Library of Congress in the spring of 1985. The Library's Preservation Testing Office was given cylinders from the collections made by several different manufacturers (Edison, U.S. Everlasting, etc.). The samples provided were chosen because of their advanced level of deterioration. After subjecting them to various heat, chemical, and atmospheric tests, it was determined that, though flammable and impossible to extinguish when ignited, even those celluloid cylinders in the poorest condition are not a fire or safety hazard. Consequently, they do not require handling, storage, or environmental conditions beyond that recommended for other working collections (70°F, 50 percent RH). When this finding was presented at a 1987 joint film/television/sound archives meeting hosted by the Stiftung Deutsche Kinemathek in Berlin, considerable reservation was expressed by Dr. Henning Schou, Chair of the FIAF's (Federation Internationale des Archives du Film) Technical Symposium. He pointed out that nitrate materials stored at temperatures as low as 40° C (104° F) for as little as three weeks will suddenly self-ignite. He explained that this was caused by the breakdown of the nitrate elements when heat builds up to and stays at 104° F for as little as three weeks (Orbanz et al., 1988, pp. 52-53).

Magnetic recordings have existed since the end of the nineteenth century, with the first successful tape recordings being demonstrated at the Berlin Radio Exhibition in 1935. Harold Lindsay built the first Ampex machine in 1947, successfully introducing the medium to the United States. From then on, the spread of magnetic tape is a matter of current history. The carrier has included bands and discs made of solid metal, as well as those that are paper-based. Today, the carrier includes various cellulose- and polyester-based bands and discs. These are coated with a wide variety of materials that can take and hold a magnetic charge. The tapes play at speeds from 15/16 to 30 ips and beyond, and have been packaged as open reels, cassettes, and cartridges.

Preservation of Sound Recordings

Once the initial problem of the recognition of materials is resolved, the principal problems of preservation can be considered. As A. G. Pickett and M. M. Lemcoe (1959) pointed out some thirty years ago, the resistance of an article to degradation is built into it at the time of its manufacture (p. 5). The basic materials used for the manufacture of most sound recordings are particularly dependent upon this parameter. Most recordings were not designed for long-term storage but for playback qualities and low-cost manufacture. However, steps can be taken to control the factors which contribute to the acceleration of degradation so that materials will last as long as possible.

The principal problems encountered with sound recordings are warpage, heavy wear, breakage, damaged edges, delamination, and microbiological deterioration. In mass-produced discs and cylinders, the single greatest problem is groove wear, particularly for such items as wax cylinders and shellac discs. For tape recordings, instantaneous discs, and for some mass-produced discs and cylinders, the greatest danger is delamination, or separation of the recording surface from its core or backing, with printthrough being a significant concern for magnetic tape. In general, problems of warpage, breakage, broken and crinkled edges, and microbiological deterioration are controllable by careful handling, cleaning, packaging, and storage.

Groove wear of discs and cylinders can be reduced significantly by proper maintenance of the playback equipment, including regular inspection of the weight, tracking, and condition of the stylus, use of the proper stylus for the groove, and regular cleaning of the item both before playing and before storage.

Prevention and control of delamination is far more difficult, since it usually has already begun before there is an awareness of active danger. Frequently, the problem is poor quality control in the manufacturing of the carrier, and it is often difficult to explain why one item is falling apart while its neighbor from original production through shelf life is in good condition. Of particular concern, since it most frequently occurs with one-of-a-kind recordings, delamination is now happening to CDs. The principal steps which can be taken to slow this process are careful handling and cleaning and proper maintenance of storage conditions—packaging, environment, and physical arrangement on the shelf. From all reports, the two most important factors are relative humidity and temperature.

There are a number of products on the market that claim to reduce surface wear and to cut down on the static electricity on the surface of the recording, thus lessening dust attraction. Other products available are designed to help remove dirt and dust buildup prior to playing. There are great reservations about applying such products to recordings, since it is not known what the long-term effect will be. Thus, with the exception of specific applications for cleaning given below, the use of such treatments is not recommended. Only in the most extreme cases, when the recording will clearly be lost or useless without the application, should treatments be used for anything other than controlled testing.

A problem in conservation of sound recordings, generally restricted to discs, is the presence of a label, affixed or embossed directly to its surface. Labels, with glue or heat-seals, inks, and dyes, raise a new set of questions regarding disc preservation:

—Will the label dissolve in the cleaning or aging process?
—Are the inks and dyes soluble in the cleaning solution?
—Will they fade in the general aging process?
—Are the various parts of the label acidic and will the acid have negative
  effects on the record, as now seems to be happening with CDs?

Experience has shown that the answers to most of these questions are in favor of preservation. The parts of the label may dissolve, but they can be protected with care in the cleaning and handling process; and the label is generally of a fairly high quality, reasonably low in acidity, and resistant to molds.

The question of the surface of CDs being destroyed by inks used on their labels was introduced in an article by James Erlichmann (1988).

Erlichmann maintains that the inks used in printing labels on CDs eat through the seal of the CD, allowing the foil that holds the encoded data to corrode, thus destroying the CD. Representatives of Sony and Phillips respond that, where adequate quality control is exerted during the manufacturing process, no problem exists.

CLEANING OF SOUND RECORDINGS

As with most things in the field, there is very little certainty regarding cleaning. What is known is based upon trial-and-error, not upon controlled, scientific study. For example, certain procedures have worked well for this author primarily because they do not appear to harm the item. Only time will confirm these conclusions.

However, one thing is certain: playing a dirty recording, regardless of its format, is one of the most damaging things one can do to it. Dirt is ground into its surface, where it creates abrasions and unwanted variations in the playing surface. These, in turn, cause distortion in the transmitted signal, complicate and exaggerate the aging process and, in extreme cases, actually obliterate the signal and prevent its being read. One should not assume that new recordings are clean. Almost certainly they are not. The only proof one needs for this is to wipe the surface of a new recording with a soft, clean, white cloth. Any item that is to be played should be cleaned first. Likewise, any item to be stored should be cleaned prior to packaging and storage. Otherwise, enough damage can be done to prevent future retrieval of an acceptable signal.

There are several successful methods for cleaning sound recordings. The mechanical techniques available include ultrasonics, vacuum machines, and, for buffing, abrasion. Of course, there is always cleaning by hand. The custom-built ultrasonic machines for cleaning discs are at the Swedish Radio in Stockholm and at the Library of Congress in Washington, D.C. (This author has not seen an ultrasonic machine for cleaning tape.) The disc is secured on the cleaning machine's turntable, cleaning liquid is applied through a cleaning brush, the solution is worked into the grooves of the disc by the brush via rotating the turntable, and the liquid and debris that are loosened are removed by a vacuum device built into the machine. Vacuum machines for discs are manufactured by a number of firms, such as Keith Monks, Nitty Gritty, and VPI. All work well to very well, but reviews of VPI say that it gives among the best service while maintaining an excellent maintenance record for the money. The laser-disc cleaners also work quite well. In these, the disc is secured to the turntable, a buffing solution is applied by hand, and the disc is moved back and forth in a stroking motion while being buffed by a pad built into the lid of the machine. The buffing cleaners for tape used in most archival collections and professional recording studios place a roll of a paper material called *pellon* on a roller moving at opposite directions of the tape to be cleaned. As the tape is wound onto its take-up reel, it moves against the pellon and is cleaned by it.

If the only means available for cleaning is by hand, this should be done very carefully. Most recordings, when hand-cleaned, should be gently wiped with a clean, soft, lint-free cotton velvet cloth or cleaning brush moistened with the cleaning agent. The cleaning is done in a circular motion (going with the grooves) for grooved discs, in a spoke or radial direction (going across the grooves) for laser discs, and for the length of the tape for magnetic tape.

The type of cleaning solution used depends upon the recording to be cleaned, the material(s) of which it is made, and the dirt and debris to be cleaned from its surface. Whether it is a solid or a laminated object must also be taken into consideration. Except in emergency situations, one should avoid cleaning fluids containing alcohol for all recordings. In any case, alcohol should not be used on shellac discs, since various kinds of alcohol dissolve shellac. Although alcohol does not dissolve polyvinyl chloride, the primary ingredient in vinyl discs, some experts caution against its use on LPs because of the threat of the loss of plasticizer or stabilizer. Also, because of the wide variety of materials used in their manufacture and the possibility of a breakdown of the bond between their surface and base, alcohol should not be used to clean laminated recordings, discs, tapes, or cylinders.

Conservators at the Library of Congress use freon TF for really dirty items, for most tape materials, and for most acetate materials. The Library uses a solution such as the DiscWasher D4+ for vinyl records and D4+ Shellac Formula for shellac recordings, in a four-to-one solution with distilled water. This cleaner is used whether the recording is being cleaned by a vacuum machine or by hand. Alcohol is used only in extreme cases, with normal cleaning following. Extreme care must be used with the application of any liquid to laminated recordings, particularly those with a wood or paper base, for the base will expand if it gets wet, causing the recording surface to warp and break even faster than normal.

Routine stylus and tape head cleaning must accompany any record cleaning procedure. The best way to clean a stylus is to use a specially designed stylus-cleaning brush with short, tightly packed bristles, such as those from DiscWasher or LAST. Another acceptable method is to use an ultrasonic stylus cleaner, such as those from Signet or Hervic. The manufacturers of such ultrasonic devices recommend that they be used in conjunction with cleaning fluids which they furnish. The author is not aware of any reported problems with this procedure or of independent analysis to determine if there is reason not to follow these recommendations. Tape heads are cleaned by hand, using cotton swabs and either freon TF or alcohol. Demagnetizing of the heads is carried out at the same time.

Once a recording has been cleaned, it should *not* be put into the same dirty container from which it was taken. If the container must be kept because of historical or content information, it should be cleaned carefully and an inner sleeve or liner used with it. Paper inner sleeves should be avoided because the paper breaks down over time and contaminates the surface and/or grooves of the recording with paper debris. An inner liner chemically similar or identical with the item should be avoided because like items, particularly plastics, tend to adhere to one another. According to some reports, materials similar in composition allow stabilizers or plasticizer to migrate between the items. Thus, polyvinyl sleeves should not be used because they are too much like the polyvinyl of LP records. Instead, an inner sleeve made of or lined with high density polyethylene or polyurethane, as are available from such firms as DiscWasher, V.R.P., and Mobile Fidelity, is recommended. For disc storage where the original jacket is not retained, the author recommends a sleeve of polyethylene-foil-paper board based on Pickett and Lemcoe's recommendations (1959, p. 48). The Library of Congress has developed specifications for such a package which it purchases from Shield Pack, Inc., of Monroe, Louisiana.

The question of package design for cylinders, wax and celluloid alike, is still unresolved. The original boxes are too high in acid to be acceptable, and to manufacture the same design today in an archival material has, thus far, been too costly. All alternate designs which have been suggested have one or more problems. The design presently used by the Library of Congress (a rectangular box whose top and bottom are folded into inward facing pyramidal shapes to support the cylinder from the inside) answers many of the problems, such as keeping the cylinder upright, preventing its surface from coming into contact with solid objects, and making it expandable to accommodate varying heights. In addition, the design protects against dust reasonably well and is comparatively inexpensive. However, if closed too tightly, the top and bottom will act as a wedge which easily splits the particularly fragile and brittle recordings. Also, the inner surface must be lined with polyvinyl and foil to give a smooth surface, to prevent paper debris, and to give a temperature barrier. Further suggestions for solving this particular problem are especially needed.

For many years, the only option available for packaging tape recordings was the container in which they came. As an outgrowth of another problem dealing with availability of containers for film, the National Archives and the Library of Congress asked the National Bureau of Standards for suggestions on the chemical makeup of containers for magnetic tape. They suggested a chemically inert material which could be shaped into the desired package—polypropylene plastic with an antimony oxide fire retardant. Carbon black or titanium dioxide are the acceptable coloring agents. The container so designed has a UL fire rating of V-2, which is reasonably good and much better than almost all other available plastics. It is very strong (able to hold a 200-pound weight without being crushed or broken) and has many of the design features which Pickett and Lemcoe recommend (1959, p. 61). Their suggestions are gradually being realized in future improvements in the design of the container, as well as solving problems with keeping the lid closed. A variation of their recommendation on storing the tape in a sealed poly/foil container is now being made for the Library of Congress by Shield Pack. This container, which will store film materials, is being considered for use with the polypropylene box for long-term storage of magnetic tape.

The Storage Environment

One of the major concerns in the conservation of all media is the environment in which they are stored: temperature, relative humidity, light, and cleanliness. Sound recordings are no exception. Two basic facts should be taken into consideration when considering the storage environment: an item will generally double its predicted life span for every 10°C the storage temperature can be lowered, and the optimum temperature and RH for the growth of the majority of mildews is 79-82°F with a 70 percent RH and over. The recommendations Pickett and Lemcoe made in the 1950s for working collections are still accepted: 70°F, 50 percent relative humidity (p. 45). General discussions for RH appear to be leading toward lowering the desired environment to 35 percent (plus or minus 5 percent) with tape storage aiming at an even lower reading of 20 percent. The present recommendation for long-term, archival storage to be as cool as possible but above freezing goes well beyond the Pickett-and-Lemcoe-suggested 50°F. All agree that environmental stability is essential, and that any significant cycling of either the temperature or the relative humidity, much less both, will cause major problems in the future. Also, where at all possible, all sound recordings should be stored in a darkened room, away from sunlight and artificial lighting of the shorter wavelengths.

The actual shelving units used should allow discs and tapes to stand vertically. Dividers should support the recording from top to bottom and from front to back. These should be attached in such a way as to be sure that they will not slip accidentally and they should be placed at regular intervals of not more than five inches apart. This ensures that the recordings remain vertical and do not lean against one another or against the shelving. Units must be sufficiently strong to support the fairly substantial weight of recordings. The properly packaged LP records required to fully load a 36-inch by 70-inch shelf unit will weigh over 500 pounds; an equal quantity of 78s weighs over 820 pounds. Cylinders should be stored standing on their ends.

Digital Signals on Optical Discs

A very exciting event in information conservation and preservation that is taking place today is the use of digital signals on optical discs. Even though not all are directly related to audio, a restatement of the advantages of this comparatively new system is warranted. The disc is read by lasers, so no physical contact comes between the stored data, wearing it out faster than its own built-in properties dictate. The disc has the capability to store aural, visual, and machine data in a digital mode, thus preventing loss of data in the transfer from one generation to another.

The realm of the laser disc is still so new that its problems are only beginning to be understood. Nonetheless, several generalities can be made. Laser discs should be stored in the same vertical position as any other disc; they appear to respond favorably to the same temperature, humidity, and environmental conditions as other discs; their surfaces need to be protected from dirt, scratches, and abrasions; and they should be handled with care.

As with all new media, there are still a number of questions to answer and problems to resolve with the optical disc. Among them are the following:

—What is the potential life of the package?
—How important are fluctuations in heat and humidity to their long-term stability and successful data retrieval?
—Is light of particular wave lengths a significant factor in their deterioration and, if so, are they the same ultraviolet wavelengths that should be avoided with other plastics?
—Will the clear surface scratch easily or discolor because of age, heat, humidity, and/or light?
—Will any of the various components of the package—plastics, inks, various metals—interact to break down the package and/or shorten its anticipated life?
—Under what conditions will the laminated disc separate?

A number of very real problems have begun to surface with laser discs. Among them are "laser rot" (a situation where the image begins in good condition, and then, over time, deteriorates into what has been described as "technicolor confetti" by Woodcock [1987]); delamination of the various strata of the disc; and deterioration or destruction of the pits which carry the data, reportedly because the seal of the discs is penetrated by acids in the ink used to print the label. These phenomena are, thus far, only rarely encountered. The industry reports that all such laser disc problems are caused by poor quality control during the manufacturing process and not by flaws in the design or its various component parts.

One thing to keep in mind is that equipment used in making instantaneous digital audio recordings is not yet standardized. Specific to this, the Association for Recorded Sound Collections' Associated Audio Archives (ARSC/AAA) took the following position:

> ... the combination of digital audio recorders, magnetic recorders using magnetic tape, and digital formats is not appropriate for the generation *of archival preservation transfer copies* of sound recordings at this time [March 1987] for the following reasons:
>
> 1. There are no nationally accepted Standards for the various digital recorders and formats.
> 2. The audio industry has yet to resolve its conflicting systems.
> 3. Neither equipment nor formats have yet been tested or proven reliable in an archival setting for making archival preservation transfer copies of sound recordings. (ARSC, 1987, pp. 13-14)

When the industry and the various national and international standardization bodies do come to agreement, particularly so for the instantaneous, write-once digital disc, and presuming the shelf life is acceptable, digital recording will become the preferred archival rerecording and storage standard. Until that time, librarians and archivists must support the ARSC/AAA position and take a wait-and-see attitude for digital signals for archival storage.

CONCLUSION

One of the major problems which must be faced when dealing with sound recordings is the wide variety of forms and the even wider variety of materials of which they are made. As technology continues to evolve, an even greater problem is the speed of which formats, materials, and equipment become obsolete. Thus, an archival collection finds itself needing to acquire and stock not only the carriers of the information sought and the equipment which will allow the "reading" of this information but also the spare parts and the mechanical expertise to keep that equipment in working order. Some suggest that the solution is to rerecord all recordings onto whatever is the standard of the day. This is totally unfeasible, if for cost alone. For example, if the Library of Congress were faced with rerecording each of the 80,000-plus audio items it received in the last twelve months alone, the cost would be well over $6,000,000 just for blank tape and engineers' time. Rerecording of its entire audio collection would cost close to $200,000,000. Further, at the rate format and equipment change, another rerecording of each of these items could be anticipated within the next ten to twenty years. Additional expenses in such a project include space to house the new copies, staff to handle and maintain the collections, and adequate environment to store them in a manner that will ensure their physical existence until the next rerecording takes place. Finally, there is the single most costly thing which collections face: catalog control.

Obviously, some materials must be rerecorded to ensure that their information will last. To undertake such a costly action because the industry wants to bring a new technology onto the market, especially one for which they themselves have not yet adopted standards, seems foolish and extravagant. Further, it seems only reasonable that the preservers of our cultural heritage must realize the sizeable contribution they make to the profits of that industry, and take an active stand for reason in what appears to be an ever-increasing evolution of new technologies. These technologies offer minimal, if any, improvements upon the preservation, conservation, organization, storage, or dissemination of collective knowledge.

Clearly, the solution cannot be to endlessly rerecord holdings. A more permanent storage medium must be sought and an archival format accepted that will be good for fifty years or more. Further, since the job is far too large for any one or two collections to undertake, collections must coordinate research efforts into the various factors that affect the long-term storage and retrieval of the data and materials in multiple collections. Building a shared pool of knowledge is necessary to prevent the premature loss of archival items and, thus, loss of the knowledge of human civilization. Only in that manner can it be ensured that such information will be transmitted to future generations.

The Association for Recorded Sound Collections' Associated Audio Archives Committee (ARSC/AAA), a group consisting of participating representatives from fifteen of the major sound archives in the United States, has begun working together toward these ends. Their recently completed two-year audio preservation planning study, carried out under a grant from the National Endowment for the Humanities, is documented in an 862-page report now available from the ARSC. The report is a preliminary working reference document and consists of a summary and three appendices. Appendix I contains more than sixty major conclusions and recommendations. Appendix II contains a detailed description of the project and the eleven individual research assignments carried out by project participants. The portion of the report dealing with storage and handling, for instance, contains a thirty-one page outline, an index of storage and handling factors, and an annotated bibliography on library construction. Other topics covered in greater or lesser degree include documentation, relevant standards, bibliographic control, dissemination, consortia potential, technical considerations, education and training, legal questions, priorities, disaster preparedness, and a professional organization for sound archivists. Appendix III consists of several compilations: a 50-page preliminary glossary, a 137-page index of terms, the responses of more than thirty-five sound archives to a resources questionnaire sent out during the project, and a bibliography of over 2,500 citations relevant to audio preservation.

The ARSC/AAA is now preparing a proposal that, if funded, will support it in the preparation of a soup-to-nuts handbook on sound archiving. To be compiled from the collective institutional knowledge and experience of its members representing over 200 years of professional experience with sound archives, the handbook will also help to highlight those areas where there is inadequate documented information. From this will come both a codification of recommendations and a series of controlled studies to gain the knowledge needed to continue. Also anticipated is the offering of workshops to be carried out by the staff for ARSC/AAA members, as well as an ongoing publication program to ensure that the knowledge gained in the process is available to all who wish to use it.

ACKNOWLEDGEMENTS

The author is particularly grateful to Merrily Smith, Chandru Shahani, and Robert McComb of the Library of Congress Preservation Office for assistance on the chemical and technical matters; to the Library's Safety Officer, Steve Bush, on matters concerning health and safety; and to two members of his staff, Larry Miller and George Kipper, for information on handling and cleaning.

APPENDIX A

Addresses for Companies Cited

DiscWasher
1407 N. Providence Rd.

Columbia, MD 65205
(314) 449-0941

Hervic Electronics, Inc.
14225 Ventura Blvd., #204
Sherman Oaks, CA 91423
(213) 789-0368

Keith Monks Audio Lab (KMAL)
c/o Allied Broadcasting Equipment
Richmond, IN
(317) 962-8596

The LAST Factory
2015 Research Dr.
Livermore, CA 94550
(415) 449-9449

Nitty Gritty Record Care Products
4650 Arrow Highway #F4
Montclair, CA 91763
(714) 625-5525

Plastic Reel Corporation of America (PRC)
Brisbin Ave.
Lyndhurst, NJ 07071
(201) 933-5100

Shield Pack, Inc.
2301 Downing Pines Rd.
West Monroe, LA 71291
(318) 387-4743

Signet
4701 Hudson Dr.
Stow, OH 44224
(216) 688-9400

V.P.I., Inc.
P.O. Box 159
Ozone Park, NY 11417
(718) 845-01034

APPENDIX B

Cylinder Storage

The recommended storage for cylinders is given below:

1. Handle the most common-sized cylinders by inserting two fingers (middle and index) into the cylinder, spreading them just enough to hold the cylinder securely. The larger diameter "grand" or "concert" cylinders should be held by inserting four fingers into the cylinder while placing the thumb on the edge or rim. Only touch the cylinders from the inside or on the extreme edges since touching the sound grooves deposits oil and grime into the sound modulations.

2. Avoid sudden changes in temperature. Allow a cylinder to adjust to room temperature (approximately 70°F) before handling it, if at all possible. Even the heat from a hand may crack a cylinder. Always allow it to come to room temperature before playing.

3. Store cylinders at a constant temperature of 55°F, 50 percent RH.

4. Store cylinders in an upright position—on edge, not on the grooved surface—in such a way that they will not be exposed to sudden jolts or shocks.

5. Container used should be closed in such a way as to make a reasonably dust-free seal. (Some cylinders were sold wrapped in cotton batting. This was intended to protect the recording while in transit, never for long-term storage. Over time, the wrapping often has adhered to the grooved surface. Once this happens it is almost impossible to remove completely. Cylinders with such materials still around them should have the materials carefully removed.) Store celluloid cylinders separate from all others, making sure that their cartons and storage cabinets have good circulation to allow the escaping gases to dissipate.

APPENDIX C

Disc Storage

The following procedures are recommended for the storage of discs:

1. Store cleaned disc recordings in a sealed sleeve made of a laminate of polyethylene-paperboard-foil-polyethylene of a heavy, acid-free paperboard which is lined with a soft aluminum foil of 0.001 inch thickness and polyethylene. The discs should not be packaged and sealed until they are properly cleaned and are in equilibrium with the intended storage area. If it is determined that the recording should be stored within its commercial sleeve, use an inner sleeve made of or lined with high density polyethylene or polyurethane.

2. When handling a recording or when placing it in its sleeve, never touch the playing surface, either with the hands or with the surface of the sleeve or its liner. Instead, hold the disc between the fingers and the thumb, with one or more of the fingers in the center and the thumb on the outside of the disc. The sleeve should be slightly bowed as the recording is slid in.

3. Stack temperature should be maintained at 70°F and 50 percent plus or minus 5 percent RH for often-used recordings, and 50°F and the same RH for seldom-used recordings.

4. Storage, playback and packaging room/s should be dust-free and at the recommended temperature and RH for often-used recordings. Discs exposed to other environments should be conditioned in the playback area for twenty-four hours prior to playback and for an equal period in the storage area atmosphere before being returned to storage.

5. Store in a darkened room, where possible, but always away from sunlight and from artificial lighting of the shorter wavelengths.

6. Store all discs in the vertical position without pressure on the surface and without the opportunity for off vertical attitude, using only clean, unabrasive surfaced packaging as suggested in item one above; do not permit sliding contact of disc surface with other surfaces.

7. If a disc is to receive heavy playing, particularly if it is unusual or unique, rerecord it as necessary to prevent undue wear and destruction.

8. Remove any "shrink wrapping" type of wrapping materials from the records and their containers.

APPENDIX D

Magnetic Tape Storage

The recommended storage for all magnetic tape, regardless of the signal which is carried, or the thickness, width, or packaging, is as follows:

1. Where possible, use only reel-to-reel tape, on the largest possible, unslotted hubs, whose flanges are immediately replaced if they are deformed out of plane.

2. Package reels in sealed metal cans or sealed boxes of a material such as polyethylene-cardboard-foil-polyethylene laminate or a chemically inert plastic. The boxes should be stacked on edge on the shelves. Tape should not be packaged until it is in equilibrium with the stacks.

3. Stack temperature should be maintained at 70°F and 50 percent RH (plus or minus 5 percent) for often-used recordings, and 50°F and 30 percent RH (plus or minus 5 percent) for seldom-used and particularly valuable recordings.

4. Playback and packaging rooms should be dust-free and the same 70°F, 50 percent RH as the stacks. Tapes exposed to other environments should be conditioned in the playback environment before playback.

5. Stray external magnetic fields should not be permitted in the stacks, playback, and packaging areas. The maximum flux density should be 10 gauss.

6. Playback equipment should be carefully maintained as recommended by the manufacturer, including cleaning, tape transport adjustment, and component demagnetization.

7. A rewind-and-inspection deck, separate from playback facilities, should be used for packaging, cleaning, and inspection. Winding tension for 1.5 mil polyester tape should be a constant torque of 3-5 ounces at the hub of a 10-inch reel.

8. The best tape presently available for storage purposes has a 1.5 mil polyester base. Chromium-dioxide (CrO_2) tape has been having major stability problems and should be avoided until the problems are completely resolved.

9. Tape should be recorded at a maximum level below 2 percent harmonic distortion (4dB below normal recording level is usually satisfactory). The first and last fifteen feet of the tape should not be used for program

recording, but should have a burst of 10 mil wavelength (approximately 760 cps at 7.5 ips) signal at maximum recording level, preceded and followed by several layers of blank tape for inspection purposes.

10. Tape should be aged in the packaging room for six months prior to recording. Recorded tape which has been exposed to other than the prescribed environment should be conditioned in the packaging room for six weeks prior to packaging.

11. Storage shelves should be free from vibration and shock.

APPENDIX E

Weight and Space Requirements for Audio Materials

The following is the average weight of the formats and the approximate count of each format per linear foot when properly packaged. Figures are based upon a random sampling of the audio collections at the Library of Congress.

FORMAT	WEIGHT PER ITEM	NO. OF ITEMS PER FT
LPs	0.51	66
45rpm	0.22	66
16″ vinyl	0.6	66
16″ acetate	0.9	66
78 rpm	0.83	66
CD	0.25	29
cylinders	0.27	3.6
audio cassettes	0.30	18
10″ audio-tape	1.77	13
7″ audio-tape	0.73	15

APPENDIX F

Recommended Storage Material

The National Bureau of Standards recommended material for storage containers of present tape and film based materials is as follows:

MATERIAL: inert homo- or co-polymer polypropylene.

DENSITY: 0.94 g/ml or higher at 25°C.

IZOD IMPACT: 1.5 ft-lbs / inch of notch for a 1/8 inch specimen (ASTM D256A).

TENSILE YIELD STRENGTH: 3,800 psi (ASTM D638).

FLEXURAL MODULUS: 125 at 1,000 pst (ASTM D790).

FLAME RETARDANT: ethylene bis(disbromonorbornanne) dicarboximide of 3.0 percent to 4.0 percent.

UL FLAMMABILITY RATING: V-2 or better.

ANTIOXIDANT: distearyl thiodipropionate (DSTDP) of 1.0 percent or less.

COLORING AGENT: Carbon black or titanium dioxide only.

REFERENCES

Association for Recorded Sound Collections. Associated Audio Archives Committee. (1987). *Audio preservation: A planning study*. Silver Spring, MD: Association for Recorded Sound Collections.
    (Note: Final performance report, NEH grant PS-20021-86. Made possible by a grant from the National Endowment for the Humanities. Consists of a summary and three appendices with more than 60 major conclusions and recommendations. Topics covered include storage and handling, documentation, standards, bibliographic control, dissemination, consortia potential, technical considerations, education and training, legal considerations, priorities, disaster preparedness, and a professional organization for sound archivists, a preliminary glossary (fifty pages in length), the responses of more than thirty-five sound archives to a resources questionnaire sent out during the project, and a bibliography of over 2,500 citations. Available from Elwood McKee, 118 Monroe St., Apt. 610, Rockville, MD 20850.)
Davies, W. E. (1980). Close-up view of record wear. *Audio, 64*(9), 38-42.
Erlichman, J. (1988). Compact discs 'fade out after eight years' use. *Guardian*, June 29, 1.
    (Note: A summary of the breakdown of CDs due to penetration of the seal.)
Fontaine, J.-M. (1987). *Degradation de l'enregistrement magnetique audio: Processus de deterioration de l'enregistrement analogique*. Paris: Phonotheque Nationale.
Geller, S. B. (1983). *Care and handling of computer magnetic storage media*. NBS special publication, v. 500-101. Washington, DC: National Bureau of Standards.
    (Note: Cover information states "Issued June 1983, I Final report. S/N 003-003-02486-4, item 247 (microfiche)." Includes bibliographical references.)
Orbanz, E.; Harrison, H. P.; & Schou, H. (1988). *Archiving the audio-visual heritage: A joint technical symposium, Federation Internationale des Archives du Film, Federation Internationale des Archives de Television, International Association of Sound Archives*. Berlin: Stiftung Deutsche Kinemathek.
    (Note: Contains thirty papers presented at the conference of the same name in the International Congress Center, Berlin, organized by Stiftung Deutsche Kinemathek, May 20-22, 1987.)
Pickett, A. G., & Lemcoe, M. M. (1959). *Preservation and storage of sound recordings: A study supported by a grant from the Rockefeller Foundation*. Washington, DC: Library of Congress.
    (Note: An independent study of the causes and possible cures of the breakdown of sound recordings commissioned by the Library of Congress.)
Brown, D. W.; Lowery, R. E.; & Smith, L. E. (1984). *Prediction of the long term stability of polyester-based recording media*. Washington, DC: National Bureau of Standards.
    (Note: NBSIR 84-2988. Preliminary report prepared for the National Archives.)
Information Systems Consultants, Inc. (1985). *Videodisc and optical digital disk technologies and their applications in libraries: A report to the Council on Library Resources*. Washington, DC: Council on Library Resources.
Woodcock, R., & Wielage, M. (1987). Laser rot. *Video, 2*(4), 49-52.
    (Note: Includes description of deterioration of signal on video discs and possible causes; gives partial list of some titles where problem has been found.)

GORDON B. NEAVILL

Associate Professor
School of Library and Information Studies
University of Alabama
Tuscaloosa, Alabama

Preservation of Computer-Based and Computer-Generated Records

INTRODUCTION

Half a century after the invention of printing, the German humanist and Benedictine abbot Johannes Trithemius published a book called *In Praise of Scribes* in which he fervently advocated the continued copying of books by hand. He argued that the discipline of copying was spiritually good for the monks, and he pointed out that despite the availability of printed books in large numbers, there remained many unprinted books that were worth copying. But the core of his argument was based squarely on the issue of preservation:

> All of you know the difference between a manuscript and a printed book. The word written on parchment will last a thousand years. The printed word is on paper. How long will it last? The most you can expect a book on paper to survive is two hundred years. Yet, there are many who think they can entrust their words to paper. Only time will tell. (Trithemius, 1974, p. 63)

It is now nearly 500 years since Trithemius wrote, and the era of electronic digital communication is in its infancy. The advent of the computer is comparable in its revolutionary implications to the advent of the printing press. Like printing from movable type, electronic digital communication offers significant advantages over previous technologies, and it has taken hold and spread very rapidly. As the twentieth century draws to a close, more and more records are being created, stored, and disseminated in digital form. A growing number of analog records are being converted to digital form so they can be incorporated into computer-based systems. But just as no one in the fifteenth century

45

fully grasped the implications of the printing revolution, the implications of the computer revolution—social, cultural, economic, and intellectual—remain largely unclear to us.

Especially unclear are the implications for long-term access to digitally encoded information. Issues concerning the preservation and survival of records in digital form have attracted little attention. How long will various forms of digital media last? What steps must be taken to ensure the survival of the information they contain? We have little experience or substantive knowledge to guide policy decisions concerning the preservation of computer-based and computer-generated records, but the implications of what is known are troubling. Many digital storage media have short life expectancies; moreover, retrieval of their information content is dependent on specific software and hardware that may have even shorter life expectancies. Some of the best informed computer experts believe that the only way to ensure long-term access to information is to retain it in human-readable rather than digital form.

Traditional approaches to preservation, with their emphasis on preservation of the storage medium, are largely irrelevant in an electronic environment. The challenge of preserving digitally encoded information for the use of future generations requires rethinking every aspect of the preservation problem in light of digital technologies. This article will raise questions, identify possible problems, and suggest some of the issues that will need to be addressed in the electronic age. Few solutions or specific recommendations are offered. All too often it will be necessary to echo Trithemius's "Only time will tell."

CONCEPTUAL FOUNDATIONS

It will be helpful to begin by trying to establish some conceptual foundations for the problem. Some of the following general statements and conceptual categories apply to the preservation of nondigital media as well as to computer-based and computer-generated records.

The survival of information for archival purposes in any environment depends first of all on the information technology used to capture or transmit the information. Inherent characteristics of the technology largely determine the nature and severity of the preservation problems that will arise. Second in importance are the librarians, archivists, and museum curators who select the recorded messages that will be acquired and retained by their institutions. Third are preservation specialists, most of whose efforts are directed at materials already housed in institutional collections.

Several concepts that illuminate the problem of preservation can be borrowed from communication and information theory. Communication theorists from Harold Innis (1951) to James W. Carey (1989) have explored concepts of space and time. Preservation is concerned with the transmission of information through time rather than space. Some information technologies, such as printing, are effective in transmitting messages through time and space; others are best adapted to one kind of transmission. Many of the information technologies that emerged in the nineteenth and twentieth centuries, such as the telegraph, telephone, radio, and television, are concerned primarily or solely with transmission through space. To be transmitted through time, information normally has to be captured in a documentary record of some kind. Some information technologies do not produce documentary records at all; some produce documentary records that are preservable only with great difficulty; others produce stable documentary records with long life expectancies.

Information theory as it was developed by Claude E. Shannon concerned the transmission of messages through space, but it can easily be applied to transmission through time. Shannon's concept of noise is especially relevant to the preservation of computer-based and computer-generated records. As formulated by Shannon and Weaver (1949), noise consists of additions "to the signal which were not intended by the information source. These unwanted additions may be distortions of sound (in telephony, for example) or static (in radio), or distortions in shape or shading of picture (television), or errors in transmission (telegraphy or facsimile), etc." (p. 99). The degradation of digitally encoded records over time involves the loss of information together with increases in noise that result in reading errors. Error detection and correction codes based on the principle of redundancy mitigate these errors over the short term, but eventually the signal becomes unreadable.

Sidney B. Geller (1974), in a seminal paper that appeared in *Datamation* fifteen years ago, defined information content as *hard* (fixed storage) or *soft* (variable storage). Hard content tends to alter characteristics of the storage medium irreversibly. Print on paper, patterns on film, or coded pits burnt into a substrate by a laser are examples of hard content. Soft content produces changes in the storage medium that are reversible with little or no permanent change in the medium itself. Magnetic technologies in which information content consists of magnetized domains on a ferromagnetic layer are a prime example of soft content.

In an archival system, Geller noted, it is necessary to take into account both *media decay*, the physical deterioration of the medium itself, and *content decay*, the qualitative loss of stored information.

Furthermore, two types of decay rates must be distinguished. *Static decay* is the deterioration of the medium or content as a function of time when it is not being used. *Dynamic decay* is the deterioration of the medium or content as a function of time when it is used in actual operation. Hard content in a medium with a high dynamic decay rate may have a shorter lifetime than soft content in a medium with a lower dynamic decay rate. For example, the hard content of a phonograph record that is played frequently has a shorter lifetime than the soft content of a magnetic tape recording. On the other hand, the phonograph record has a lower static decay rate than the magnetic tape. A rarely played phonograph record should last longer than tape.

Finally, Geller emphasized that, in an electronic environment, thinking about archival quality must "deal with the preservation and security of the entire system which acts as the carrier of the encoded information" (p. 72). Loss of information can result not only from decay of the storage medium but "from the loss of a unique code or decoder (such as a one-of-a-kind transducer)" (p. 72).

DIGITAL TECHNOLOGIES

Inherent Characteristics and Implications for the Survival of Information

The manuscript book that Trithemius trusted would have to be classified in Geller's terms as an example of soft content. Parchment was so tough and durable that the words could be scraped off with a knife. It was also expensive and sometimes hard to come by, so palimpsests—manuscripts written on recycled parchment—were not uncommon. No one knows how much of the lost literature of antiquity and the Middle Ages was destroyed so that parchment could be reused for other purposes.

With magnetic information technologies, we have entered the age of the electronic palimpsest. Magnetic media can be erased and reused with ease. Digital encoding of information coupled with magnetic storage carries this a step further, allowing the erasure of specific data within a record and the interpolation of new data at will. The ease with which data in magnetic digital records can be deleted, modified, updated, and rearranged in new configurations gives computer-based systems a tremendous advantage over print-based systems for the provision of current information. However, it raises serious questions about the survival of information. As this author has written elsewhere, "The malleability of information that is one of the major advantages of computer-based electronic systems has as its corollary the potential transience of information" (Neavill, 1984, p. 77).

The kinds of preservation problems that arise from the malleability of information will be clearer if magnetic digital records are compared with printed records. The information content of printed records is frozen in a particular configuration. In order to revise or correct a printed record, especially if the revisions are at all extensive, a new physical document must be generated. This is normally done by issuing a new edition consisting of multiple copies of the revised text. Copies of the old edition do not cease to exist when the new edition appears. As long as printed documents survive as physical objects, their information content is likely to survive as well.

Ink on paper (especially nonacidic paper) is an effective means of transmitting information through time. A large portion of the paper documents in libraries and archives are outdated or no longer relevant to the purposes for which they were created. Many of these documents are rarely used and remain of interest primarily to historical scholars. The fact that such documents survive as physical objects after they have served the purposes for which they were created is an inherent characteristic of paper-based information technologies. The importance of this characteristic cannot be overestimated. It is largely what makes historical scholarship possible.

In a paper-based environment, outdated city directories, maps, commercial catalogs, membership lists, and publications of many other kinds survive as physical objects and provide important retrospective information to scholars. The value of these records today derives from the fact that their content is frozen. They provide a snapshot of the way things were at a particular time in the past. Successive editions of these publications document and date historical change. For example, a collection of Chicago city directories from 1870 to 1893 would document the economic demography of the city before the Chicago fire, the devastation caused by the fire, and the rebuilding of the city up to the Columbian Exposition.

In a computer-based environment, the content of such information services would be kept continually up-to-date. There is no certainty that outdated information would be retained. Inertia, legal requirements, or its continuing commercial value may cause outdated information to be retained in some systems, as in the Bowker *Books in Print* database, where records of out-of-print books have been retained since 1979. The problem here is that outdated information is likely to be stored in a cumulative file. A cumulative file may contain current and retrospective information, as in the online version of *Books in Print*, or there may be a separate retrospective file, as in the CD-ROM version. A cumulative file provides information about specific out-of-print books, but, unless it is enhanced with costly retrospective features that are irrelevant to the commercial purposes for which the file is created, it destroys the historical context of the information. In contrast, back volumes of the printed version of *Books in Print* can answer the kind of time-specific questions that interest historians.

In an online environment, much of the retrospective documentation that is taken for granted in a print-based environment may be lost. The survival of information is a problem not only where the content of computer-based records is continually revised, but also where computer-based records may be purged from a system because commercial demand has fallen off or because they are no longer relevant to the purposes for which they were created. The loss of historical documentation, or at least the danger of this loss, is inherent in magnetic computer technologies. How serious a problem is this? Is it worth major concern?

The computer is not the first information technology whose introduction has resulted in the loss of retrospective documentation. The invention of the telephone enhanced the ease and speed of spatial communication at the cost of the survival of messages through time. Anyone who has used twentieth-century archives is aware of the dramatic decline in meaningful documentation that resulted from the adoption of the telephone in place of correspondence. Changing technologies of library catalogs provide another example. Until roughly one hundred years ago, most libraries relied on printed book catalogs that appeared occasionally in revised editions. The printed catalog was produced in multiple copies and did a good job of transmitting information about a library's holdings through space as well as time. Its successor, the card catalog, was ineffective on both counts. The compelling advantages of the card catalog were that it allowed the catalog to be kept continually up-to-date, simplified the revision of bibliographic records already in the file, and permitted more access points than were practicable in printed catalogs. In recent years, historians of books have been using printed catalogs to analyze the kinds of books that were available in particular communities in the eighteenth and nineteenth centuries. It will be difficult to carry these studies into the twentieth century. As continually updated files of current information, card and online catalogs cannot provide retrospective documentation about a library's holdings at particular times in the past.

People tend to accept information losses like these, if they think about them at all, because the losses seem unavoidable and because the advantages of the new technologies for millions of users of current information seem to outweigh their disadvantages. This response is rapidly becoming untenable. As more and more of society's records are created, stored, and disseminated in digital form, the level of potential information loss becomes far greater than anything experienced in the past. A recent study that explored problems related to the electronic recordkeeping of government information began its report with the words, "The United States is in danger of losing its memory" (Committee on the Records of Government, 1985, p. 9). It is a question of retaining contact with the past, not simply of providing grist for professional historians' mills. As Edward Shils (1981) has written, "If we could imagine a society in which each generation created all that it used, contemplated, enjoyed, and suffered, we would be imagining a society unlike any which has ever existed" (p. 34). Our inheritance from the past comprises the greatest part of the contemporary stock of knowledge. We draw on that inheritance continually to understand ourselves and our world and to generate new knowledge.

Not all magnetic digital records are subject to continual revision or destruction. Many computer-based systems are designed to collect, store, and manipulate series of historical data such as census and meteorological records. The content of these records may be augmented with new data, but older data are rarely altered or erased. This was not always true in the early years of data processing, when the possibility that future researchers might wish to manipulate data in unforeseen ways was less obvious than it is now. Raw data were not always retained after statistical summaries were prepared. Punched cards containing raw data from the 1940 and 1950 censuses were routinely destroyed, for example (Committee on the Records of Government, 1985, p. 88). Today, the importance of retaining such data is generally recognized. The preservation of digital records whose content is not in flux is not as problematical as the preservation of records whose content is subject to change.

The problems thus far discussed are associated with the soft content of magnetic technologies. They are not inherent in optical technologies, where digitally encoded information is stored as hard content in the form of coded pits burnt into a substrate. Here, information content is frozen in a particular configuration on what appears to be a relatively permanent medium. Optical data discs are written individually; in this respect they can be compared with the manuscript book. CD-ROMs (Compact Disc-Read Only Memory) are produced from a master in editions of multiple identical copies. They are comparable with print media insofar as the survival of information is concerned. When the information content of a compact disc is revised, a new edition is produced; copies of the old edition do not cease to exist.

Currently many libraries are unable to rely on CD-ROMs for retrospective information, but this is a problem that arises from the way they are marketed and is not inherent in CD-ROM technology. Many publications issued in compact disc formats are updated on a regular basis. Each new edition contains the complete database, superseding previous editions. Subscriptions tend to be expensive, so publishers commonly require subscribers to return old discs when a revised edition appears. This precludes the emergence of a secondary market in slightly outdated discs that would cut into the vendor's primary market. It also means that old editions of compact discs, unlike superseded editions of most printed reference works, may not be available in libraries and archives to provide retrospective documentation. There is no assurance that compact disc publishers retain archival copies of outdated discs or that they would permit access to them by scholars if they were retained. In order to fulfill their scholarly responsibilities, research libraries and archives will have to challenge the distribution policies of many compact disc publishers.

Two characteristics of digital technologies enhance the chances for survival of digitally encoded information. First is the ease with which digital records can be copied or converted to new formats without loss of information content. In contrast, information is lost when analog records are copied, and the losses become progressively severe with succeeding generations of copies. Second, although reading errors increase as digital records undergo static or dynamic decay, error detection and correction devices in digital records can mitigate information losses even in records that are in advanced stages of degradation. End-of-life of digital records is reached only when errors overwhelm the ability of error detection and correction devices to correct them. Without these two characteristics, it is doubtful whether digital media could be considered for purposes of transmitting information through time.

Preservation of Digital Storage Media

Two distinct technologies, magnetic and optical, are used for the storage of digitally encoded information. Data tape, hard discs, and floppy discs are examples of magnetic media. Optical data discs and compact discs are examples of optical media. Erasable magneto-optic discs combine magnetic and optical technologies.

The lifetime of magnetic storage media is measured at best in decades; optical storage media may have a somewhat longer life expectancy. In contrast, the lifetime of archival-quality paper and photographic film is measured in centuries. Digital storage media are not considered to be of archival quality (National Research Council, 1986, pp. 68, 76). In the long run, the preservation of digitally encoded records is concerned with the preservation of content rather than storage media. The preservation of digital storage media focuses on the short term, generally ten to twenty years. Here, the objective is to maintain information content until it can be copied or until the file is converted to a new format. Preservation at this level is concerned with identifying the characteristics of digital storage media that contribute to degradation, establishing conditions for storage and handling, monitoring the deterioration of storage media, and scheduling copying or file conversion. Most of what is known about the preservation of digital storage media relates to magnetic data tape. The following discussion focuses on this medium, with some tentative comments about optical media.

Magnetic data tape is subject to both dynamic and static decay. Since the tape is in direct contact with the heads of the transport when it is written and read, a certain level of dynamic decay is unavoidable. The primary problem, however, is static decay. To understand the nature of the problem, one needs to look at the composition of the tape.

Magnetic tape consists of a ferromagnetic layer bonded to a polyester base. The base is stable against environmental degradation under ordinary use (Cuddihy, 1980, p. 558). A National Bureau of Standards study found that the base, stored at 20°C and 50 percent relative humidity, should retain useful properties for 500 years (Smith, 1986, p. 2). The ferromagnetic layer is composed of ferromagnetic particles of about one micron in length. The useful properties of the tape derive from these particles. Information on the tape is stored and manipulated in terms of the magnetic qualities of these particles, whether they are magnetized or not, and the direction of the polarities. The particles themselves are chemically stable. The problem lies in the binder in which the particles are suspended. Binder formulas vary from one tape manufacturer to another, but they consist basically of polyester polyurethane to which various lubricants, adhesives, and stabilizers (against such dangers as oxidation or bacterial growth) are added. The binder is subject to environmental degradation by hydrolysis, a chemical reaction between the polyester polyurethane and atmospheric water vapor. High temperature, high humidity, and acidic pollutants in the air accelerate the hydrolytic reaction. In a new tape, the binder has a high force of adhesion to the base. As the tape ages, the adhesion drops rapidly and the binder layer becomes brittle. The weakened binder may flake off the base, and a gummy substance may be exuded. The gummy substance can lead to increased error rates when the tape is read (Bertram & Cuddihy, 1982, p. 993). Tape lifetime is limited by degradation and detachment of the binder from the base.

The National Bureau of Standards recently concluded a five- or six-year laboratory study titled "Prediction of the Long Term Stability of Polyester-based Recording Media." Data were written on tapes which were rapidly aged at known temperatures and relative humidities. Data were read after aging. Aging and reading attempts then alternated until the tapes became unreadable. The study concludes that tape lifetime is easily ten to twenty years, probably longer, under normal storage conditions and room temperature and 50 percent relative humidity. However, the authors cautioned, "There are documented reports of tape failure after ten years of storage under normal room temperature and humidity and we have seen cases of failure after only a few years so the lifetimes can vary considerably" (Smith et al., 1986, p. 1). No systematic differences were found between the commercially available tapes tested. Tapes sold as "archival" at higher prices apparently last no longer than other tapes, although they may have superior performance in other respects (L. E. Smith, personal communication, October 25, 1988).

Modern tape transports can retrieve information from digital tapes in terrible condition, including very brittle tapes, but there is an endpoint at which tapes can no longer be read. The only way to preserve the information content of magnetic data tapes is to recopy them on a regular basis, perhaps every twelve to twenty years. One of the objectives of the National Bureau of Standards study was to develop a simple, qualitative test for binder separation to help determine when a tape needs to be copied. The simplest test is apparently to crease an insignificant part of the tape and roll it between thumb and forefinger. Aged tapes often lost binder, sometimes when creased and sometimes after several passes between the fingers (Smith, 1988).

A number of guidelines are commonly suggested for tape storage and maintenance. These include sampling tapes on a regular basis for errors, checking for deterioration, cleaning and rewinding tapes every one or two years, and eventually, recopying. It is essential to create an identical copy of the original tape, preferably on tape of a different manufacturer, and to store it under good conditions in a separate facility. The National Bureau of Standards publication, *Care and Handling of Computer Magnetic Storage Media* (Geller, 1983), provides a thorough summary of current practices. There is also a useful brief article by Benjamin L. DeWhitt of the National Archives and Records Administration in *Conservation Administration News* (DeWhitt, 1987).

Floppy discs have a somewhat shorter life expectancy than magnetic tape. The National Bureau of Standards estimates that a floppy disc stored under proper conditions can provide information for ten to fifteen years; archivists estimate that information on a floppy disc may last no more than five years (Committee on the Records of Government, 1985, p. 32). Many people store correspondence files, original versions of published writings, and other personal archives on floppy discs. These archives must be copied or converted to new formats on a regular basis. Otherwise, they are likely to be lost or become inaccessible because of dependence on obsolete hardware or software.

Optical technologies are far more stable than magnetic technologies. Here we are dealing with hard content: coded pits burnt into a substrate of glass, metal, or durable plastic. The information content is read by a laser so there is no physical contact between the reading head and the surface of the disc and virtually no basis for dynamic decay. There are, however, grounds for concern about static decay. The National Research Council's Committee on the Preservation of Historic Records (1986) has noted,

> The factors of storage that are most harmful to the optical disk are heat and humidity. Humidity causes oxidation of the recording surface, and heat accelerates the process. Some of the other factors that cause concern are the adhesion of various layers one to another, catalytic corrosion, galvanic corrosion, and mechanical stresses. (pp. 73-74)

It is sometimes asserted that compact discs are virtually indestructible. One author has written that you could probably use a compact disk "to play Frisbee with your dog" (Miller, 1986, p. 22). This is fantasy; optical media have to be handled carefully. Manufacturers tend to be more conservative. Many vendors claim a life of ten to forty years for CD-ROMs, with most of the claims on the low end of that range. These claims do not appear to be based on test results or other reliable data. It may simply be a case of caution on the part of vendors who have no idea how long their products will last.

The durability of optical media is related to the materials from which the discs are made. Discs using a glass substrate with a gold alloy or platinum coating layer are the most durable. Commercially produced CD-ROMs, which use a plastic (polycarbonate) substrate with a chemically reactive coating layer such as aluminum, are the least durable. The Library of Congress has conducted accelerated aging tests of optical discs. Glass and gold alloy discs have been baked for 2,000 hours without bringing them to end-of-life. Discs are now being tested after having been baked for 3,000 hours (B. Nugent, personal communication, October 1988).

System as a Whole

The fact that digital storage media are not of archival quality is unimportant in terms of preservation. Geller (1974) noted that the term "lifetime" applies to storage media, information content, and the system, which he defined as "the total grouping of all of the interrelated components, the storage medium and the encoding/decoding schemes"

(p. 75). Little is gained if storage media outlive other components of the system, including hardware and software, that are required to provide access to their information content.

The crucial factor in the preservation of computer-based and computer-generated records is the life expectancy of the system as a whole. According to Geller, system end-of-life can be caused by obsolescence due to technological or sociological advances that make maintenance of an existing system costly and inefficient, inability of the system to perform reliably after a certain time, loss of one-of-a-kind transducers or encoding/decoding keys, or a breach in a highly secure system (p. 75). The following discussion will focus on the third category.

Electronic hardware is not expected to function for more than ten to twenty years. Generations of incompatible hardware rapidly succeed each other. When computer tapes containing raw data from the 1960 federal census came to the attention of the National Archives and Records Service in the mid-1970s, only two machines in the world were capable of reading them. One was in Japan; the other was deposited in the Smithsonian as an historic relic (Committee on the Records of Government, 1985, pp. 86-87). Successive generations of discontinued hardware cannot be maintained by manufacturers or archival institutions to provide access to superseded digital formats.

Software is also necessary for the recovery of digitally encoded data. Software tends to change more rapidly than hardware, and generations of software tend to be even less compatible than generations of hardware. There are examples of software that have gone through thirty versions in a decade. The proper operating system must be available at the time of data recovery.

Another problem is documentation of the software. Not only must the proper operating system be available, but documentation is necessary to give information about the digital codes used and the organization or format of the record. Documentation may be in machine-readable or human-readable form. It is not unusual for documentation to be incomplete or missing.

Security is a preservation issue that deserves to be dealt with at greater length than is possible here. In order to protect data, it may be necessary to encode them in more cryptic form. Higher density storage also requires more sophisticated coding and decoding schemes. In both cases, recovery of data becomes more difficult if the key to the code is lost. And, of course, the amount of information that can be lost if anything goes wrong increases with the density of storage.

The long-term preservation of computer-based and computer-generated records requires constant vigilance on the part of the archivist. Records must be copied on a regular basis to prevent loss of information due to media or content decay. In practice, most copying will involve conversion to new formats to ensure that the records remain compatible with current systems. Original software must also be preserved and copied. Documentation must be carefully preserved, ideally with the records themselves. The costs of this kind of preservation are high, but if these procedures are carried out conscientiously, they can ensure "an almost endless data lifetime" (Geller, 1974, p. 76).

The risks are high as well as the costs. In 1984, a Committee on Preservation established by the National Archives and Records Service to advise on machine-readable records issued a white paper that argued strongly against the preservation of archival records in machine-readable form (National Archives and Records Service, 1984; Mallinson, 1985b). The committee members had impressive technical credentials and represented such institutions as the Center for Magnetic Recording Research at the University of California, San Diego; IBM; the 3M Corporation; the National Security Agency; and the National Bureau of Standards. Their opposition to machine-readable archives was based primarily on problems related to hardware and software dependence. They proposed, instead, a system relying on archival quality silver halide microfilm. The advantage of microfilm mass memory is that the information content is permanently stored in human-readable form. Access to the information content merely requires magnification, not complicated decoding devices. Members of the committee met again in the summer of 1988. Despite advances in optical storage technologies, they remain strongly convinced that human-readable storage is the only kind that makes sense in an archival situation (Smith, 1988). In their view, machine-readable storage for preservation purposes is simply too risky, and it condemns the archival agency to perpetual copying and reformatting of records.

POLICY ISSUES

The preservation of computer-based and computer-generated records for the use of future generations is one of the greatest challenges facing librarians, archivists, records managers, and other members of the information community. We are just beginning to understand the dimensions of the problem. The next step will be to formulate information policies to ensure the survival of digitally encoded information. A few of the policy issues that will have to be addressed are outlined below.

The first issue to be resolved is whether records are to be retained in human- or machine-readable form. Although there are strong arguments against converting existing archival records to machine-readable form, it is unlikely that records created and disseminated in digital form will be widely converted to human-readable form for preservation purposes. Records created specifically for manipulation by machine, such as interactive fiction, hypertext, and statistical and bibliographical data files, must be retained in machine-readable form. Digital storage may not be advisable in all cases, but the problem of preserving machine-readable records cannot be avoided.

The next issue concerns the locus of responsibility for preservation of computer-based and computer-generated records. As stated earlier, the survival of information for archival purposes in any environment depends, first of all, on the information technology used to capture or transmit the information and secondly, on the librarians, archivists, and museum curators who select the recorded messages that will be acquired and retained by their institutions. Commercial and other organizations that generate and disseminate information cannot be expected to assume an archival role. Preservation is not their responsibility; in any case, they go out of business or change their policies too frequently to be reliable. If computer-based and computer-generated records are to be preserved, they will have to be preserved in institutions dedicated to that purpose.

The selection of records to be acquired for preservation purposes will be far more difficult in an electronic environment. Decisions to acquire computer-based records will have to be made before their information content is erased. Archival institutions in a print-based environment can acquire records years after their creation, when their research significance is established. Digitally encoded information that is not acquired when it is current may be lost forever. The librarians and archivists who select computer-based records for acquisition and retention will have to anticipate the needs and interests of future generations as best they can. A national information policy to ensure that essential information is preserved would be desirable.

The preservation of continually updated databases for purposes of retrospective documentation is an especially difficult problem. The best solution seems to be to download information from the database at established intervals which would provide periodic snapshots of the database with the information content frozen at a particular moment in time. The snapshots could be in whichever format is eventually accepted for archival storage. The critical issue for future scholars would be the selection of databases to be preserved.

The acquisition of computer-based records by institutions dedicated to preservation raises economic and legal issues that will have to be addressed at the national level. Fewer institutions will need to assume an archival role in an electronic environment, but responsibilities for preservation will have to be coordinated to ensure that essential records are preserved. Patterns of economic support for research libraries will have to be reordered. In a print-based environment, current publications constitute the vast majority of acquisitions at most research libraries; retrospective information needs are served in large part by materials whose original purchase was justified on the basis of their provision of current information. The economic link between the provision of current and retrospective information is broken in an electronic environment where libraries provide access to a wide range of computer-based records they do not own. Economic support specifically for the acquisition and preservation of retrospective materials will have to be increased.

CONCLUSION

As we grapple with these issues in the years ahead, we will have come full circle to Trithemius. He was in no sense opposed to the new technology of printing. He fully recognized the advantages of printing for disseminating ideas. His own books, including *In Praise of Scribes*, were printed, and his circle kept one Mainz printshop so busy that it practically became the abbey press. He was wrong about the life expectancy of the fifteenth-century printed book, but he grasped that a single technology may not be equally effective in transmitting information through both space and time. Our thinking for the past half millennium has been the product of a world where the dominant information technology accomplished both objectives fairly well. As we enter the electronic era, we must try to think again of transmission through space and time as separate issues. Assumptions derived from a print-based environment about permanence and the cumulative growth of knowledge may give way to a heightened awareness of the fragility and vulnerability of the stock of human knowledge, and a return to the unending medieval preoccupation with preservation and recovery.

REFERENCES

Bertram, H. N., & Cuddihy, E. F. (1982). Kinetics of the humid aging of magnetic recording tape. *IEEE Transactions on Magnetics, 18*(5), 993-999.

Carey, J. W. (1989). *Communication and culture: Essays on media and society.* Boston, MA: Unwin Hyman.

Committee on the Records of Government. (1985). *Report of the Committee on the Records of the Government.* Washington, DC: The Committee.

Cuddihy, E. . (1980). Aging of magnetic recording tape. *IEEE Transactions on Magnetics, 16*(4), 558-568.

DeWhitt, B. L. (1987). Long-term preservation of data on computer magnetic media. *Conservation Administration News, 29*(April), 7, 19, 28; *30*(July), 4, 24.

Geller, S. B. (1974). Archival data storage. *Datamation, 20* (October), 72-80.

Geller, S. B. (1983). *Care and handling of computer magnetic storage media.* NBS Special Publication 500-101. Washington, DC: National Bureau of Standards.

Innis, H. A. (1951). *The bias of communication.* Toronto: University of Toronto Press.

Mallinson, J.C. (1985a). The next decade in magnetic recording. *IEEE Transactions on Magnetics, 21*(3), 1217-1220.

Mallinson, J. C. (1985b). Archiving human and machine readable records for the millennia. In *Second international symposium: The stability and preservation of photographic images* (August 25-28, 1985) (pp. 60-63). Springfield, VA: Society of Photographic Scientists and Engineers.

Miller, D. C. (1986). Finally it works: Now it must "Play in Peoria." In S. Lambert & S. Ropiequet, (Eds.), *CD-ROM: The new papyrus* (pp.21-35). Redmond, WA: Microsoft Press.

National Archives and Records Service, Committee on Preservation, Subcommittee C. (1984). *Strategic technology considerations relative to the preservation and storage of human and machine readable records.* White Paper. Available from NARS, Washington, DC.

National Research Council. Committee on Preservation of Historical Records. (1986). *Preservation of historical records.* Washington, DC: National Academy Press.

Neavill, G.B. (1984). Electronic publishing, libraries, and the survival of information. *Library Resources & Technical Services, 28*(1), 76-89.

Shannon, C. E., & Weaver, W. (1949). *The mathematical theory of communication.* Urbana: University of Illinois Press.

Shils, E. (1981). *Tradition.* Chicago: University of Chicago Press.

Smith, L. E., (1986). *Prediction of the long-term stability of polyester-based recording media: Progress report to June 1986.* NBSIR 86-3474. Gaithersburg, MD: National Bureau of Standards, Institute for Materials Science and Engineering, Polymers Division.

Trithemius, J. (1974). *In praise of scribes.* (K.Arnold, Ed.; R. Behrendt, Trans.). Lawrence, KS: Coronado Press.

SUSAN DALTON

Director, Preservation & Archival Projects
National Center for Film and Video Preservation
at the American Film Institute
Washington, D.C.

Moving Images:
Conservation and Preservation

INTRODUCTION

October 6, 1993 will mark the 100th anniversary of the first U.S. copyright registration of a motion picture. It was registered under the title Edison Kinetoscopic Records, but there is no known copy of the film, nor is it known what images it contained. That this significant first in film history did not survive is not only symbolic of the fate of thousands of films in the past, but also of that which may yet await the majority of the moving images produced today. Although the chemical composition of nitrate motion picture film is inherently unstable, in many ways a greater threat to the survival of these films was the attitude of producers and public alike. Films were considered as mere entertainment with no importance beyond immediate commercial exploitation. As a result of many years of deliberate destruction, neglect, fire, and deterioration, over half of the motion pictures produced before 1951 no longer exist.

Today, there is an awareness that moving images are the most vivid and compelling records of history and are a powerful force in shaping culture. While this heritage must be preserved, the challenge of doing so is enormous. An estimated 90 million feet of uncopied nitrate film in U. S. archives has yet to be preserved—and there are millions of feet of fading color films; thousands of unprotected independent, educational, industrial, and amateur films; and vast quantities of unpreserved television news and entertainment programs. If even a portion of these moving images are to be safeguarded, there must be an awareness of the scope of the problem and a recognition that the responsibility for preservation is shared by producers, archives, libraries, historical societies, and film and video study centers. Every institution holding moving images has an obligation to protect this material for future generations. Every year, more and more institutions are recognizing their own role in what is—and must be—a national preservation effort.

The movement to archive films began in the United States with the pioneering efforts of the Museum of Modern Art (MoMa). MoMA began in the 1930s to collect and preserve films as works of art and was a founding member of the International Federation of Film Archives (FIAF) in 1938. The National Archives and The International Museum of Photography at George Eastman House soon joined in the preservation effort. The Library of Congress, which received films as copyright deposits until about 1912, began to acquire films for the motion picture division in the mid-1940s and established a preservation program in 1958. Although the efforts of these archives were considerable, much of early cinema had already been lost.

In 1967, the American Film Institute began a nationwide effort to locate and acquire nitrate films for preservation. To assist in this effort, the National Endowment for the Arts established the AFI/NEA Film Preservation Program to fund the conversion of nitrate film to safety stock. Over the next twenty years, many thousands of early films were saved through the combined efforts of the major archives. Over 21,000 nitrate films were acquired for the AFI Collection at the Library of Congress alone. But the problem of moving image preservation grew with the times. Archives became more and more concerned about the many other types of unprotected films and the problems presented by the preservation of television programming. The National Center for Film and Video Preservation was founded in 1983 and continues the activities of the AFI Archives Program in the areas of film acquisition and the publication of the *AFI Catalog of Feature Films*. The Center is committed to serving as an instrument of national coordination and is designing and implementing a National Moving Image Database (NA-MID) which will eventually provide data on film and television holdings at archives, studios, and networks as a tool for preservation.

The need for coordination in moving-image preservation has been recognized for many years. In the late 1960s, major institutions involved in nitrate preservation established the Film Archives Advisory Committee (FAAC) in order to avoid duplication of efforts and to ensure that the best possible copies of films were being preserved. In the late 1970s, institutions involved in television preservation formed a similar group (TAAC), and eventually the two were combined into the Film and Television Archives Advisory Committee (FAAC/TAAC). FAAC/

TAAC is an informal organization, with no constitution, no rules and regulations; all institutions with film or video collections are invited to join. Meetings are held once a year and are attended by individuals from about seventy institutions. Presentations on topics of interest, such as technical developments in film and television preservation or standards for cataloging of moving image materials, are always included in the program. FAAC/TAAC also has working groups devoted to special purposes, such as independent film and television news. The National Center serves as the secretariat for FAAC/TAAC and publishes a quarterly newsletter on archival activities. (More information on FAAC/TAAC is available from the National Center for Film and Video Preservation at the American Film Institute, P. O. Box 27999, 2021 North Western Avenue, Los Angeles, CA 90027. Their phone number is (213) 856-7637).

PRINCIPLES OF PRESERVATION

The dictionary states that to preserve means to keep safe from injury or harm; to keep or save from decomposition; to keep alive, intact, or free from decay (Webster's New Collegiate Dictionary, 1973, p. 910). To preserve a film or videotape, it is certainly necessary to safeguard it from chemical or magnetic destruction; and, since the "moving" of moving images is provided by equipment which can damage or destroy them, they must also be protected from unwarranted use. Thus the preservation of a film or videotape cannot be considered secure unless a master copy is held by an archive. This is a general principle which has been advocated by the International Federation of Film Archives (FIAF) and one to which the major archives in the United States subscribe.

In practice, this principle means that moving images should not be used as reference copies until master material is preserved in a public institution. In these days, when video outlets abound throughout the country, the need to be so concerned about preservation may seem a bit remote. However, many times in the past a shrunken, scratched, and overprojected print has proved to be the only copy of a Hollywood feature that was once distributed nationwide. Locally produced films or television programs have an even greater chance of being unique and unprotected copies.

The first step in any archival program is to identify the material and determine its preservation status. It should be noted here that it is extremely unwise to identify films by running them on a projector.

Using hand rewinds and a manually driven viewer (or magnifying glass) is the only truly safe method.

Any unique films should be protected by negatives or master positives; copies of unique videotapes should be made for reference use. All original materials should be retained whenever possible and should be stored under appropriate archival conditions. In addition, any film or videotape—even if it is not a unique copy—needs special care and storage.

Film

Although some rare development processes have been used for motion pictures, the images in most films are formed from the reaction of silver halides with light. The silver halides undergo a chemical change when exposed to light; an image is formed in the development process and is then fixed to make it permanent. The basic structure of film consists of three layers: the image layer, composed of a gelatin emulsion in which the silver halide crystals are suspended; the substratum or binder (sometimes also called the adhesive or substrate layer) which enables the emulsion to adhere to the third layer, known as the support or base. All three of these components present problems for conservation and preservation, but the problems presented by the base will be the main concern here. (The preservation of color films is the subject of another presentation and will not be addressed in this report).

Cellulose Ester Films

Esters are simply compounds which are formed by the reaction of an acid and an alcohol. Most film bases are esters of cellulose, a naturally occurring substance found in cotton, wood fibers, etc. Cellulose ester base is manufactured in a process known as solvent casting in which cellulose fibers are esterified with acid (a preparation usually referred to as the "dope") and combined with other ingredients such as plasticizer and fire retardants (Sargent, 1974; Lee & Bard, 1987, 1988). This mixture is then dissolved in alcohol and spread on a heated, rotating drum. The heat causes the alcohol to evaporate, and the result is a thin sheet of transparent film which can be stripped off the drum and prepared for emulsion coating. Cellulose ester films are named according to the type of acids used in the manufacturing process, i. e., cellulose nitrate, cellulose triacetate, and so forth.

All layers of motion picture films are hygroscopic, that is, they absorb moisture. If too much moisture is absorbed, the film undergoes hydrolysis and begins to break down. On the other hand, if conditions are too dry, the plasticizer compounds, which provide flexibility, can evaporate and the film will shrink, buckle, and become brittle. In addition, the chemical composition of each type of cellulose ester film causes particular problems.

Nitrate Film

Cellulose nitrate film —in which the cellulose was esterified with nitric and sulfuric acids—was the standard for 35mm theatrical motion picture film from the beginnings of the motion picture industry until 1951. There is a great deal of published information about nitrate film and many people are familiar with its characteristics even if they have not handled it personally.

Although it is a surprisingly strong and durable substance, nitrate film is chemically unstable and deteriorates in a process which is both inevitable and irreversible. Nitrate is also highly flammable. It is not explosive, but deteriorated film has been shown to self-ignite at temperatures as low as 106°F. Once ignited, a nitrate fire burns extremely rapidly and is impossible to extinguish. Burning nitrate also gives off toxic fumes which can be fatal if inhaled.

Decomposition of nitrate film really begins from the date of its manufacture. Obviously, this can be a very slow process since there are films over eighty years old which are still in good condition.

However, unless a means to arrest the decomposition process is discovered—which is unlikely—all nitrate film will eventually completely deteriorate. Storing nitrate film properly enhances its longevity, thus buying time to copy it onto a more permanent medium.

In the first stage of nitrate decomposition, the image begins to fade or discolor and the film begins to emit a pungent odor. As the process advances, the emulsion begins to soften and the film becomes brittle and sticky. The image then disappears entirely and the film becomes either a solid, almost glasslike mass or, sometimes, a viscous black sludge. Ultimately, the film degenerates completely into an acrid brown powder.

Any films in the last stages of deterioration should be considered hazardous and should be placed under water in steel drums or other suitable containers until they can be disposed of properly. However, it should also be noted that sometimes a thin layer of nitrate powder can appear on top of a film which is otherwise in good condition. It is also possible to mistake rust from the film can or reel for nitrate deterioration. One should not become alarmed and throw films out by mistake.

As nitrate decomposes, it releases nitrogen oxides which accelerate the decomposition process and can harm other nitrate and acetate films in the area. Decomposition is also accelerated by heat and humidity. The film must therefore be stored in cool, dry conditions with sufficient air circulation so that the gases released do not accumulate. Nitrate should be stored in a segregated area with its own air supply so that nitrogen oxides cannot affect other films.

The generally recommended temperature for archival storage of nitrate is between 35° and 50°F., with a humidity range of 40 to 50 percent (Bard et al., 1983). It is difficult to achieve low temperatures without increasing relative humidity, so some institutions have had to be satisfied with a temperatures somewhat above 50°F in order to maintain a humidity level of not more than 50 percent, but in no case should nitrate be stored at a temperature of more than 70°F. Fluctuations in temperature and humidity should also be avoided. Experience has shown that when films have been subjected to wide fluctuations in temperature and humidity, they can begin to deteriorate very rapidly. Newly acquired films which have been exposed to such fluctuations during shipping should therefore be inspected frequently, and all nitrate film should be inspected at least once a year. Inspection involves more than just opening the can. Each reel should be wound slowly from end to end and, if deteriorated sections are found, the film should be copied immediately. If this is not possible, the deteriorated sections should be cut out to keep them from infecting the rest of the reel.

Nitrate storage must also conform to fire codes and meet established safety standards. A few reels may be kept in fireproof cabinets, but any substantial quantity of nitrate must be stored in a specially constructed vault. Most institutions do not have such facilities and rent space in commercial vaults. Organizations with only a few reels of nitrate may be able to find space on a cooperative basis with one of the major archives. (More detailed information on regulations for storing nitrate is available from the National Fire Protection Association in Quincy, Massachusetts.)

It is illegal to send nitrate film through regular mail, but if packed and labeled according to regulations, it may be shipped via Federal Express, UPS, and other surface and air transport. As a flammable solid, nitrate is classified as a hazardous material and regulations for packing and shipping may be obtained from various transport companies. Nitrate should not be shipped in the summer or at anytime when the outdoor temperature is above 70°F. Nitrate in an advanced state of deterioration should *never* be shipped. Again, film in this condition should be placed in a container filled with water until it can be disposed of properly. One should consult with local fire authorities for regulations about proper disposal.

One of the problems with 35mm film is that it is not always easy to determine if it is on nitrate stock. For many years, some manufacturers printed the words "nitrate film" along the edge, but not all films from all manufacturers were marked in this way. Unmarked nitrate can be identified by dropping a small clip into a bowl of trichlorethylene; however, trichlorethylene has been classified as a carcinogen, so this method is now rarely used.

Some people resort to the burn test, i. e., to clipping a very small piece of the leader or a tiny strip from along the edge and lighting it. If used, this test should always be done out of doors and never near the reel of film in question. In general, for all 35mm films which are known to be produced prior to 1952, it is best to treat them as nitrate until they are identified otherwise (Eastman Kodak, 1969). Although some 16mm films on nitrate base have apparently been found, 16mm film was never manufactured in the United States on nitrate base and the chances of running across it are extremely slim.

Acetate Film

The term *acetate* is often used generically to describe all safety film, but in fact, there are several kinds of acetate film such as cellulose diacetate, cellulose acetate propionate, and cellulose triacetate. Work to develop a nonflammable film was begun very early and a safety base film was available in 1908. Early safety films were not suitable for commercial purposes because they were neither strong nor flexible enough to stand theatrical use and they had poor geometric stability, i.e., they shrank, often dramatically. Safety film was therefore confined to educational and amateur use and was manufactured in 9.5mm, 28mm, and other nonprofessional gauges. Some of these nonstandard gauges are a special problem because of the scarcity of equipment on which to copy them. 16mm film, introduced in 1923, remains in common use today.

The most common problem of early safety film is that the plasticizer has been lost to such an extent that the film is far too brittle to withstand projection and sometimes cannot even be unreeled without breaking into pieces. It can also become so shrunken that it curls into a tube shape, making it nearly impossible to copy.

Early safety film, diacetate in particular, often exhibits an even more serious problem in that it can disintegrate in a manner not unlike nitrate—the image fades, the base softens, and the emulsion separates from the base, giving the film a "crazed" or cracked appearance. Sometimes a deposit of white powder is formed. This usually means the film is undergoing autocatalytic hydrolysis and has absorbed moisture to the point where it begins to break down. The acetic acids used in the esterification process are released and, as acid is produced, the process of disintegration continues at an ever faster rate. Films disintegrating in this way exhibit a characteristic odor of acetic acid, which has given rise to the name for the problem: the *vinegar syndrome.*

Cellulose Triacetate Film

Cellulose triacetate film first became available for widescale commercial use in 1948. It had the strength, flexibility, and dimensional stability required for commercial use, and the manufacture of nitrate film was discontinued in 1951. Cellulose triacetate is an archival medium and is used for virtually all preservation copying. Tests have shown that, if properly stored, cellulose triacetate should last for hundreds of years.

Recently, however, examples of vinegar syndrome in triacetate film have been found which have caused concern among the archivists (Brems, 1988). Thus far, vinegar syndrome has been found to be a particular problem in hot and humid climates. It is, therefore, reasonable to associate vinegar syndrome with poor storage conditions. Since most institutions often receive films which have been stored under adverse conditions, it is necessary to recognize and guard against the problem. There are a number of research projects currently underway to identify the causes of vinegar syndrome and, if possible, to find a way to stabilize the deterioration process. However, until we know more about the process of acetate deterioration, the only hope for films exhibiting vinegar syndrome is to copy them onto new stock. Films with vinegar syndrome should also be isolated since the vapors given off can infect other films as well. Since evidence indicates that humidity may be the most important factor in causing vinegar syndrome, the humidity level of storage areas should be carefully controlled.

While proper storage has always been a basic component in archival preservation, recent concern about all forms of chemical decomposition has made archivists even more aware that proper storage is absolutely essential for the preservation of moving images. Generally recommended standards for archival storage of black-and-white motion picture film are no more than 70°F with a humidity range of 30 to 50 percent.

Polyester Film

Polyethylene terephthalate (PET) film, usually simply called polyester, has been an alternative to triacetate film for a number of years. Polyester was invented in 1941. It was developed for use as a film base after World War II and is widely used for small gauges such as 8mm and also for professional 35mm film. Polyester is also the standard support layer for videotape.

Since polyester is insoluble in most common solvents, this film base must be manufactured in a process known as *melt casting* (Sargent, 1974; Lee & Bard, 1987, 1988). Molten polyester is extruded onto a casting cylinder and then stretched in both width and length and "set" by heating. Studies have shown that polyester base has a stability equal or superior to triacetate film.

Polyester film has been proposed by many experts as the ultimate answer to film preservation. However, it has a number of drawbacks which have thus far made archivists shy away from it. One difficulty is the inability to splice it using conventional solvent methods; it must be spliced using either tape or an ultrasonic splicing device. It can also exhibit a phenomenon known as "core set" in which the film sets into an irreversible curl after having been wound around a narrow core in storage.

A more difficult problem is that the majority of films manufactured today are color stocks and most archival work is done in black and white. Appropriate negative and positive emulsions are not easily available in black-and-white polyester stock. In addition, polyester film originally presented problems in the adhesion of the emulsion to the base and, while the emulsion coating technology has improved since polyester film was first introduced, many archivists are not yet confident that the emulsion will adhere to the base on a long-term basis. Since polyester is an exceptionally strong material, it presents an attractive alternative to triacetate film for commercial use, and no doubt many films on polyester will be coming into archives. For the present, most archivists feel that more research on the adhesion characteristics of polyester needs to be done before it can be accepted as a standard for archival work (Brems, 1988).

Videotape

To many film archivists, videotape is extremely frustrating—one cannot simply hold it up to the light to see what images it contains. And herein lies the root of the difficulties for its preservation. Since videotape is not a human-readable material, it is totally dependent on appropriate equipment to retrieve the sounds and images it carries. Videotape is not considered an archival medium for several reasons. It can be very easily erased or altered. Moreover, the surface of the tape itself is abraded each time it passes over the heads which read the information. Videotape is also a relatively new medium and it has not been demonstrated to be a permanent one. Finally, experience has already proven that, even if videotape itself were to last hundreds of years, it would far outlast the equipment on which to play it.

Videotape was first introduced as a professional recording medium in 1956. In physical structure it consists of a thin substrate or base layer of polyethylene terephthalate (PET). On top of this base is a polymeric binder layer (usually from a class called polyester polyurethanes) in which magnetic particles are embedded. Some tapes also have an additional layer called backcoating, a polymeric binder in which carbon particles are imbedded.

Videotapes are subject to various forms of defects such as drop-out, a loss of picture or sound information in certain areas of the tape; print-through, in which information on one layer of the tape is transposed onto an adjacent layer in the tape pack; and various technical problems such as timing errors made at the time of recording. Many defects in videotape tapes are caused by physical damage from dust and dirt or creases in the tape caused by uneven winding. To avoid some of these defects, tapes should be used and stored in a clean environment. Tapes should also be stored on edge in a container which supports the tape reel at its hub, and should be wound slowly from end to end before storage.

Both the base and binder layers of videotape are subject to physical degradation from hydrolysis, which can cause the molecular structure of the polymeric materials to break down. Recent research also indicates that the binder is particularly susceptible to degradation when exposed to high humidities (Calmes, 1988).

The optimum recommended storage for videotapes is 60°F with a relative humidity of 25 percent. Since it is sometimes difficult to control humidity, storing tapes in vapor-tight bags may be an alternative. However, not enough is yet known about the properties of videotape cassettes and other containers and how these might affect the tape in micro-environment storage. In the meantime, storage conditions should follow the recommendations as closely as possible with an emphasis on maintaining low humidity. In addition, if tapes are used under different conditions from which they are stored, they should be allowed to equilibrate in the use environment before playing.

Whatever the problems presented by videotape composition, a far more serious difficulty is the great variety of incompatible tape formats and the growing obsolescence of the equipment on which to play them. In some cases, equipment for formats less than ten years old is not only already hard to find but also extremely difficult to maintain because spare parts are not available. Manufacturers do not continue to support the technology of outdated formats and, as technology and equipment become more sophisticated, this problem will continue to grow.

In order to preserve the information on videotape, it seems that there is little choice for the archive except to conserve tapes in proper storage and copy them onto newer formats every ten to fifteen years or so. An alternative to continued recopying of videotape, albeit an expensive one, is to copy videotape once—onto film. The technology for motion pictures is relatively simple; even in the event that film becomes an outmoded format, it should always be possible to construct projection equipment. Each archive will have to weigh the one-time expense of making film copies versus the continued expense of recopying from tape to tape. Another consideration is that in the current analog recording method, quality is lost with each succeeding generation. Digital recording holds the promise that tapes may be copied over indefinitely without loss of quality, but increasing complexity of the equipment is bound to create more problems in regard to availability and maintenance. In this sense, digital recording may be both a blessing and a bane.

Optical Disc Recording

Optical disc recording at first seemed to indicate that it would be the answer to permanent preservation for the archive. However, discs themselves are not a proven archival medium, and there have already been some examples of physical deterioration. Moreover, the problem of technology is even more vexing than that of videotape. There are over ten incompatible formats in current use, and it is to be expected that things will get more, not less, complicated. Storing moving image information on discs is excellent for quick reference and retrieval, but it cannot be considered an option for permanent preservation at this time.

CONCLUSION

The cost of film and video preservation is high, ranging from about one dollar and up per foot of film to $100 and up for each hour of videotape. This makes it all the more necessary for the archive to ensure that it is getting the best possible quality in its preservation masters. There are only a few commercial labs in the United States which specialize in copying nitrate and/or problematic safety film. Recommendations about them may be obtained from the National Center or one of the major archives. Many commercial labs can assist with general film or video copying, but if a particular lab has no experience in archival copying, it is wise to work closely with lab personnel to ensure standards of quality.

The task of preserving moving images is a difficult one and requires time, effort, and money. The problems to be faced are serious ones and the situation, particularly in regard to technology, is not getting any better. Hopefully, one day the perfect preservation medium for all moving images will be developed. In the meantime, archivists must continue to do the best they can with the materials at hand. Through the combined efforts of many institutions cooperating on a national level, it is possible to meet the challenge of preserving our moving image heritage.

REFERENCES

Bard, C. C.; Jones, C.; Kurtz, P. T.; Mutter, P. J.; Perry, R. S.; Preo, P. H.; Ryan, R. T.; & Waner, J. M. (1983). *The book of film care.* Rochester, NY: Eastman Kodak Company.

Brems, K. A. H. (1988). The archival quality of film bases. *Society of Motion Pictures and Television Engineers (SMPTE) Journal, 97*(12), 991-993.

Calmes, A. (1988, July 28-29). *Minutes of the meeting of the National Archives and Records Administration Advisory Committee on Preservation, ad hoc Subcommittee on Preservation of Video Recordings.* Washington, DC: NARA.

Eastman Kodak Company, Motion Picture Film Department. (1969). *Storage and preservation of motion-picture film.* Rochester, NY: Eastman Kodak Company.

Lee, W. E., & Bard, C. C. (1988). The stability of Kodak professional motion-picture film bases. *SMPTE Journal, 97*(11), 911-914.

Lee, W. E., & Bard, C. C. (1987). The stability of Kodak professional motion-picture film bases. *Image Technology* (December), 518-521.

Sargent, R. N. (1974). *Preserving the moving image* (G. Fleck, Ed.). Washington, DC: Corporation for Public Broadcasting and the National Endowment for the Arts.

BIBLIOGRAPHY

Bertram, H. N., & Cuddihy, E. F. (1982). Kinetics of the humid aging of magnetic recording tape. *IEEE Transactions on Magnetics, 18*(5), 993-999.

Brown, D. W.; Lowery, R. E.; & Smith, L. E. (1986). *Predictions of long-term stability of polyester-based recording media.* National Bureau of Standards Institute Report 86-374, Progress Report to June 1986. Washington, DC: National Bureau of Standards.

Camras, M. (1988). *Magnetic recording handbook.* New York: Van Nostrand Reinhold.

Increasing the life of your audio tape. *Journal of the Audio Engineering Society, 36*(4), 232-236.

Isesaka, K.; Nakamura, T.; Takahashi, S.; Kobyashi, K.; & Leader, S. (1989). The application of high-coercivity cobalt iron oxide tape for digital audio recording. *SMPTE Journal, 98*(3), 168-172.

Parson, D. (1987). *Videotape conservation and restoration: Usual defects, possible remedies.* (Minutes and working papers of the FIAT/IFTA 6th General Assembly, Montreal, 29 September-1 October, 1986)(pp. 34-49). Madrid: International Federation of TV Archives (FIAT/IFTA).

Spottiswoode, R. (1969). *The focal encyclopedia of film & television.* Great Britain: Focal Press.

Webster's new collegiate dictionary. (1973). Springfield, MA: G. & C. Merriam Company.

Wheeler, J. (1983). Long term storage of videotape. *SMPTE Journal, 92*(6), 650-654.

Young, C. (1989, July/August). Nitrate films in the public institution. *American Association for State and Local History Technical Leaflet.* Nashville, TN: AASLH.

SUSAN GARRETSON SWARTZBURG

Preservation Librarian
Rutgers University Libraries
New Brunswick, New Jersey

Preserving Newspapers: National and International Cooperative Efforts

INTRODUCTION

A newspaper, as defined by the United States Newspaper Program, is "a serial publication which is designed to be a primary source of written information on current events connected with public affairs, either local, national and/or international in scope" (Harriman, 1984, p. 2). In short, a newspaper is printed, appears at regular and frequent intervals, and concentrates on current events. The evolution of the newspaper is closely related to the development of print, which enabled people to communicate news and views far more widely than was possible in manuscript form. Because of this ability, newspapers have been, and are, controversial; the power of the press is a force to be reckoned with, if not feared. The newspaper is not a passive entity; it is at the center of a vortex of activity. It is also ephemeral, in that it is purchased, read, and disposed of within the course of a day. Because newspapers are ephemeral, many scholars have discounted their usefulness, failing to recognize that "the very unreliability of the newspaper is an important record of its environment. Newspapers not only record events with unique immediacy and impact, but they also preserve sociocultural attitudes and biases in their historical context" (Mills, 1981, p. 464). In his keynote address at the International Symposium on Newspaper Preservation and Access held in London in 1987, Sir Denis Hamilton, former Editor-in-Chief of the *London Times*, observed that the elite papers of the world are courageous because they present news and views and do not bow to public opinion (Hamilton, 1988, pp. 13-19).

Historians have always turned to newspapers to see how events were interpreted at the time that they occurred. Now, more than ever, with an increased interest in social history and in the daily life of the common person, historians have come to appreciate and use this most important element of the historical record. Thus, the questions of preservation and access have become more critical. As preservation and access are achieved, scholars are able to increase their study of people and events through an examination of the primary source of information and observation: the newspaper.

THE PROBLEM OF PRESERVATION AND ACCESS

Until a little over a hundred years ago, most newspapers published in the United States and around the world were printed on rag fiber paper; those that have survived the ravages of humans can survive for generations to come. The Industrial Revolution of the nineteenth century brought increasing literacy and an increasingly sophisticated technology for the production of paper and for printing. By the late 1860s, rag fiber was no longer used exclusively for the production of newspapers but was mixed with other chemically treated fibers of straw and ground wood. The use of untreated ground wood pulp, containing lignin, the intrinsic enemy of paper, and alum rosin sizing, which was highly acidic, for the production of inexpensive paper to be used for the publication of newspapers and "mass market" books was common practice in the United States and Europe by the 1880s. This paper is especially susceptible to heat, humidity, and light, which cause a catalytic effect that essentially causes the paper to devour itself—to disintegrate. It is ironic that one of the first historians to accept newspapers as a historical resource was John Bach McMaster (1892), whose text, *A History of the People of the United States,* was undertaken at precisely the period when the source material itself was of such poor quality that its survival for even a generation was questionable (Mills, 1981, p. 464).

By the turn of the century, the few librarians and archivists who attempted to collect and maintain newspaper files realized the impermanence of this material. As early as 1897, the Librarian of Congress recognized the problem and recommended that publishers be required to print some rag copies for library deposit as part of the copyright regulations (p. 467). Although binding and wrapping newspapers in acidic paper and storing them in darkened areas offered some protection from the ravages of temperature, humidity, and light, it was evident that some newspapers had deteriorated beyond use within a few years of their publication. Frank P. Hill, Librarian of the Brooklyn Public Library, addressed the American Library Association on the subject at its 1910 conference. His talk prompted the Association to appoint a special committee to study the problem and investigate possible solutions (Hill, 1910, pp. 299-301). By 1927, the *New York Times* began to print rag paper editions for libraries, and several other newspapers followed suit, but the practice ended with the advent of World War II and the shortage of paper (Mills, 1981, p. 467).

By the early 1930s, the U.S. government recognized the problem of rapidly deteriorating newspapers. An examination of newspapers published in the United States from 1830 to 1900 was undertaken by B. W. Scribner (1934) at the National Bureau of Standards. His investigation documented the shift in the manufacture of newsprint paper from rag fibers to untreated groundwood pulp, and his report offered suggestions for the preservation of newspapers through lamination with japanese tissue or cellulose acetate sheeting. Although these lamination processes have not proven to be very successful, demonstrating yet again the need for caution when approaching any treatment technique that promises to be *the* solution to the problem of embrittled materials, a number of his comments in the report are prescient. For example, he pointed out that "reproduction in miniature appears to be the ideal means of preserving newspaper records" (p. 10). In conclusion, Scribner observed,

> It is recommended that a coordinated effort be instituted at once by library and scientific organizations to find the most practicable means for the perpetual preservation of the newspaper records; that the perfection of materials and methods for reproduction in miniature be given primary consideration; and that consideration be given to a central agency for supplying reproductions of newspapers and other records to libraries. . . . (p. 10)

Microphotography has indeed proven to be the key to the preservation and access of newspapers, but its development for preservation purposes has been slow. The process was developed in 1850; the first newspaper was reduced to film three years later—the *London Evening News*, microfilmed to demonstrate the process (Mills, 1981, pp. 468, 483). However, the first commercially used automatic microfilming machine, marketed by the Recordak Corporation (a division of Eastman Kodak), was not available until 1928. Although it was developed for the filming of records, newspaper librarians recognized its application for newspaper microfilming and approached Eastman Kodak. The process was tested at the New York Public Library in 1933. In 1934, the Recordak Corporation introduced a fast and efficient camera and the first commercial microfilm reader. By 1935, the New York Public Library had begun to film its back files and the *New York Herald-Tribune* began the current filming of its files. Within three years, eight other newspapers had followed suit (p. 468).

The Library of Congress established its photoduplication service in

1938; by 1942, the service oversaw a full-fledged newspaper preservation program which eventually became self-supporting. Keyes Metcalf, who had been instrumental in developing the New York Public Library newspaper microfilming program, became the Director of Harvard University Library in 1937 and initiated a foreign newspaper microfilming program there which sold copies to about thirty other institutions. Microfilming, however, was not widely accepted; a survey of 112 libraries undertaken in 1940 found that only one institution had converted from the binding of newspapers to microfilm, in spite of the fact that most newspaper publishers left little margin for binding and that a bound newspaper volume was bulky and unwieldy (Jacobus, 1948, p. 295).

Following World War II, the library community again addressed the problem of newspaper preservation. In 1947, the Association of Research Libraries (ARL) formed a Committee on Microfilming Cooperation; it focused its attention on newspapers, where the need was most urgent. In 1948, it produced *Newspapers on Microfilm: A Union Checklist*, published by the Library of Congress, which established a Microfilming Clearing House the following year. T. F. Mills (1981) observes, "By 1950, a full century after the invention of microfilm and after nearly two decades of pioneering efforts and publicity, the medium had become the accepted method for preserving newspapers" (pp. 469-470). In 1952, the American Library Association established a Committee on Cooperative Microfilming Projects, making its first priority the microfilming of newspapers. ARL recognized the limitations of the Harvard effort to film and market foreign newspapers and established the Foreign Newspaper Microfilm Project in 1956. Administered by the Center for Research Libraries, the Project took over the housing of Harvard's master negatives and began to film a hundred current titles. In recent years, the Foreign Newspaper Microfilm Project has turned its attention to the problem of retrospective files of foreign newspapers.

With the proliferation of newspaper microfilming projects, there was a decline in the quality of the microfilming. Problems included high reduction ratios and uneven lighting, inadequate preparation of original materials, careless filming (a major research library discovered a roll of filmed material with a hand placed in the center of each frame), and the filming of incomplete files when complete files were available elsewhere. In 1951, the American Library Association's Committee on Photoduplication emphasized the need to maintain quality standards for newspaper microfilming, but it was not until 1972 that the *Specification for the Microfilming of Newspapers in the Library of Congress* was published, following a decade of efforts that had been undertaken with greater or lesser success. The haphazard nature of preservation microfilming being undertaken by institutions throughout the country was, and is, of serious concern to librarians, archivists, and historians.

By 1978, there were over 70,000 American and foreign newspapers known to be preserved in microform in the United States (Mills, 1981, p. 472). It took forty years to achieve that total, yet little more than a quarter of the estimated 250,000 titles published in the United States alone had been microfilmed. It was evident that accelerated efforts were urgently needed if thousands of newspapers were not to be forever lost in the following forty years. The effort needed coordination to ensure that filming would be undertaken in a systematic way, that there would be adequate bibliographic control, and that the filming would be of standard quality.

THE UNITED STATES NEWSPAPER PROJECT

By the 1960s, historians and researchers increasingly expressed concern about the inadequacy of guides to newspaper resources and the deplorable state of such resources when they were located. In 1965, a Joint Committee on Bibliographical Services to History, consisting of representatives from historical associations, libraries, historical journals, and bibliographers, was established to address these problems. The deficiencies in Winifred Gregory's (1937) *American Newspapers, 1821-1936: A Union List of Files Available in the United States and Canada* were reported at the committee's Belmont Conference in 1967; a revision of the list was identified as a priority by the Organization of American Historians (OAH). In 1971, the American Council of Learned Societies (ACLS), at the behest of the National Endowment for the Humanities (NEH), polled its membership to identify the most needed program for the preservation of research tools for scholars. OAH recommended a program to organize, preserve, and make available United States newspaper resources (Woods, 1988, pp. 4-5).

OAH received a two-year grant from NEH to conduct a survey to determine the need for a revision of Gregory and the problems associated with such a project. The results of the survey demonstrated that there was, indeed, a universal need for a revision of Gregory, and that working on a state-by-state basis through a single statewide coordinator was the most logical way to proceed, as a large percentage of newspapers were found only in the state of their origin. Most important, this survey showed what a massive undertaking such a project would be (p. 4). NEH recognized early on that libraries would play an important role in such a project. The development of the MARC (Machine-Readable Cataloging) format in the late 1960s and the establishment of the Online

Computer Library Center (OCLC) in the early 1970s provided the technical facility for the development of a national newspaper database. The CONSER (Cooperative ONline SERials) Program, begun in 1976, provided the bibliographic standards, quality control, and coordination necessary for such an undertaking. The Library of Congress began to catalog its newspaper collection in 1974 and began to incorporate these records into the CONSER database by 1975. However, newspaper records have special requirements. It was clear that the task of providing bibliographic control of newspapers was beyond that which the Library of Congress could accomplish alone.

In 1976, OAH established an office at its headquarters to implement a two-year pilot project in Iowa to "test the feasibility of operating in a state and to explore the use of computerized records" (Field, 1988, p. 8). The Iowa Project underscored the need for accurate information on the extent and quality of previous bibliographic efforts (Model, 1978). By 1978, NEH was persuaded that a long-term program, to last a decade or more to assure the preservation and access of all United States newspapers, would succeed. NEH became the coordinator of the program, a role "extraordinary for the Endowment, a body used to funding projects rather than organizing and providing ongoing management" (Sullivan, 1986, pp. 159-160). The United States Newspaper Program was formally established in 1982. Its guidelines for the project, *Procedures and Standards for U.S. Newspaper Projects*, was issued in 1985. This is

> a coordinated national effort to identify, to preserve, and to make available to researchers a significant portion of the newspapers published in this country since the seventeenth century. The projects are carried out on a state-by-state basis (including the U.S. territories) and in national repositories, such as the American Antiquarian Society and the New York Public Library, which hold titles from nearly all fifty states. (Field, 1986, p. 5)

In the fall of 1982, NEH awarded six grants to national repositories of newspapers, including the American Antiquarian Society, the Center for Research Libraries, the Kansas State Historical Society, the New York Historical Society, the State Historical Society of Wisconsin, and the Western Reserve Historical Society, to provide the initial database. Shortly thereafter, Rutgers University and the New York Public Library were added to the group; both institutions had achieved substantial control over their holdings, which were national (even international) in scope. By May 1983, sixteen planning grants were awarded, and full cataloging grants were awarded to Montana and the Virgin Islands (Sullivan, 1986, p. 160).

Today, the United States Newspaper Program (USNP) funds state-wide projects to survey newspaper repositories and to assess the status of bibliographic control and preservation of the collections. Newspaper repositories, including libraries, archives, historical societies, even private collections, are inventoried and unique titles are cataloged according to the *Newspaper Cataloguing Manual* (Harriman, 1984). The physical condition of each file of newspapers is reviewed and action is taken to ensure the preservation of its content. This activity has proven to be time-consuming, but it is essential if the newspapers are to be preserved. Preservationist Pamela W. Darling has observed, "In the long run, what good is a bibliographic record, fully tagged, coded, subject to complete authority control, accessible through a dozen search keys on a thousand terminals, if the item it represents is no longer usable?" (Smith & Merrill-Oldham, 1985, p. 103).

The preservation of a state's newspapers is a shared effort between the public and the private sector. The preservation phase of the U.S. Newspaper Program has led to a combined effort of national, state, and local initiatives. While NEH provides considerable funding for each state's Newspaper Project, it is hoped that each state can provide up to 50 percent of the cost. This can include grants from state libraries and historical commissions as well as service-in-kind from the institutions participating in the project. Funds are also provided, upon occasion, from local agencies and from the newspaper publishers themselves, who are often represented on each state's Newspaper Project Advisory Board. Although New Jersey only began the preservation phase of its Newspaper Project in 1990, threatened files have been saved with funds from both the State Library and the Historical Commission, as well as from the communities themselves and the publishers of the newspapers. It is hoped that the preservation phase in every state will bring about a combination of public and private initiative to preserve their documentary heritage.

While NEH will ensure that newspapers in danger of imminent destruction will be filmed and thus preserved, newspapers that are at present stable may not be filmed at this time. Priority must be given to newspaper files that are in greatest jeopardy because of their physical condition. NEH will support efforts to preserve original newspaper files when that option is feasible. The American Antiquarian Society has made an effort to collect, microfilm, and preserve in original format newspapers published through 1875, but this excludes material published when paper was its most fragile.

There are presently twenty-three active state newspaper projects underway; thirteen have been completed. Representatives from each of these projects meet once a year to share information and to address several problems, ranging from the sublime to the ridiculous, that can and do arise during such an undertaking. Newspaper files have been saved from the streets, from barns where a variety of creatures have nested in them, and from unscrupulous dealers who are not eager to have a unique title filmed prior to its sale (Corlis & Brown, 1988, p. 13). Each state approaches the project in a somewhat different way; certainly the author's own state's (New Jersey) problems are quite different from those of Montana. Over 4,500 newspapers have been published in New Jersey since 1777, far more than the output of such states as Montana and Washington, and more than the national output of such countries as New Zealand, Norway, and Sweden.

As has been mentioned earlier, not every United States newspaper will be saved in original format. While the remains of every newspaper might be preserved through a variety of techniques, ranging from polyester encapsulation to the physical strengthening of each individual sheet by use of delicate conservation techniques, the cost of such an effort would be astronomical. It would be well into the twenty-first century before such an endeavor to physically preserve the over 250,000 United States newspapers could be completed. Deacidification technologies, such as the Wei T'o and Diethyl Zinc (DEZ) processes, will retard deterioration but cannot strengthen paper. While efforts are underway around the world to develop techniques that will both deacidify and strengthen paper, it is likely to be several years before one or more of these techniques can be employed in a "mass treatment" situation at reasonable cost. The solution is to film endangered newspaper files as promptly as possible.

INTERNATIONAL EFFORTS

The United States is by no means the only nation to recognize the need to preserve its newspapers. In 1980, the International Federation of Library Associations and Institutions (IFLA) Section on Serial Publication established a Working Group on Newspapers to consider all matters relating to newspapers in libraries. Presently, it is working on guidelines for the cataloging of newspapers and is engaged in a survey of preservation policies of newspaper collections worldwide. Robert Harriman of the Library of Congress is the U. S. representative to the Working Group. As the United States and such former colonial powers as Great Britain, Germany, and the Netherlands began to address the problems of preservation and access to their own newspaper collections, it became evident that their national libraries often held the most complete files of newspapers published in their former colonies. It was clear that issues of preservation, bibliographic control, access, and microfilming of newspapers needed to be addressed and resolved within an international forum. Thus, the Working Group sponsored an International Symposium on Newspaper Preservation and Access, held in London in August 1987, prior to the IFLA Conference in Brighton, England. The stated aim of the Symposium was "to gather together for the first time all those concerned with the task of maintaining and preserving an invaluable research and educational resource—newspaper collections." Its intent, according to the promotional brochure, was to "provide a forum for the discussion of common concerns among those representing the major international newspaper collections of the world, their producers and conservators." Librarians gathered from four continents to discuss their approaches to the mutually shared problem of the preservation and access of newspapers.

There clearly is a need for internationally accepted policies and procedures clarifying what to preserve and how best to do so. Several questions must be resolved. For example, is a national repository responsible for preserving, on microfilm and/or in original format, every edition of every paper? How should bibliographic control be effected for such material? The questions of how newspaper collections can best be housed and how newspapers can be restored are complex ones which depend upon a number of variables in each country, such as the physical nature of the paper that the newspaper is printed upon, the environment in which newspaper collections are now housed and shall be housed, and the financial and human resources available for preservation and access. Representatives from a number of nations were shocked to learn that librarians in the United States do not attempt to preserve the original of every one of the country's 250,000 newspapers. While preservation microfilming is the accepted technology for preservation and access, many librarians are convinced that the original should be preserved somewhere, somehow.

There was considerable discussion at the Symposium about mass deacidification and paper-strengthening processes. The British Library Newspaper Library uses the Wei T'o system to deacidify individual sheets of newspapers when necessary. The French Conservation Center in Sablé is developing a deacidification procedure based upon the Wei T'o system. While newspapers are microfilmed before deacidification, much conservation work needs to be undertaken prior to filming because the originals are to be preserved. This makes the preservation process slow and labor-intensive. Dr. Gerhard Banik, former Director of Conservation at the Austrian National Library, described that institution's efforts to develop a "mass" technique for the preservation of original newspaper files; while this strengthening technique has potential, it is, to date, too expensive for practical use.

The discussion about mass deacidification and strengthening processes continues; however, there is little that is actually known about these processes, and none are in regular operation. In a session on conservation at the Symposium in London, Banik pointed out that the developers of deacidification processes have been loathe to have them scrutinized by an independent agency and have published little solid technical information about them. There is a critical need for independent review and evaluation before librarians can make rational decisions about the physical preservation of their newspaper collections. This evaluation should be similar to but considerably greater in depth than the report by the U. S. Congress Office of Technology Assessment on the deacidification and strengthening processes that include Diethyl Zinc, Wei T'o, and several others being developed in the United States (U. S. Congress, OTA, 1988). It was, and is, acknowledged that the evaluation of the Wei T'o and Diethyl Zinc processes by George Cunha (1987) was a courageous beginning. Although there were deficiencies in Cunha's effort precisely because the technical information necessary for a thorough evaluation of the processes under review was not readily available to him, he revised it in 1989 to include more information about other processes currently being developed. There is hope that Cunha's effort marks the beginning of an open sharing of information between developers and between nations on mass preservation processes. Early reports from the British Library on a technique that uses enzymes for strengthening are encouraging. The Library has a commitment to share with the world its testing of the process, which is being undertaken at the University of Manchester.

Several companies in the United States are poised to introduce their processes to librarians and archivists. While their efforts to develop a mass technique for the deacidification and/or strengthening of brittle paper are to be applauded and supported insofar as possible, the custodians of collections need to remember that many of these processes will physically change the nature of paper, which is the object to be conserved. This is not necessarily a bad thing, despite the conservator's golden rule to do no treatment unto an object that cannot be reversed, if one considers that such a treatment may indeed be the only way to preserve an embrittled newspaper in a format resembling the original. However, it is clear that these processes need to be studied very carefully to ensure that, in the long run, they will not compound the preservation problem. Reports on mass deacidification and/or strengthening techniques are beginning to appear in the library literature. While these efforts can be greeted with cautious optimism, librarians and archivists with a firm grounding in the history of conservation must insist on technical data if they are to determine which processes will be best for the mass treatment of collections. Each process has its strengths and weaknesses. Curatorial decisions about what is the appropriate treatment for each collection will have to be made. There is no right or wrong treatment. As much as possible needs to be known about each process so that educated decisions can be made. The preservation of the world's cultural heritage cannot afford national chauvinism or entrepreneurial secrecy.

Preservation microfilming, even in those countries where originals are preserved, is, at this time and in the foreseeable future, the way to ensure both preservation and access to newspapers. Rapidly deteriorating newspaper collections cannot wait until a mass treatment process is developed, tested, and proven safe over a long period of time. And the ultimate key to the preservation of the world's newspapers is cooperation.

PRESERVATION MICROFILMING

Today's Solution to the Preservation of and Access to Newspaper Collections

While the Library of Congress, the British Library, and several other national libraries are exploring optical disc technology and how it might be applied to the problem of the preservation and access of newspapers, it is clear that optical technology, presently in its infancy, is not an appropriate medium for the preservation of newspapers at this time. The currently developed technology has not proven its permanence, nor has there been an attempt, in the midst of a rapidly developing technology, to determine guidelines for playback and transfer of data. Imagine a scholar in the twenty-first century, working away in a warehouse in Maryland which the Smithsonian has constructed to house the vast number of optical readers developed in the final quarter of the twentieth century. The report, *Preservation of Historical Records,* (1986) by the Committee on Preservation of Historical Records, National Materials Advisory Board, and the Commission on Engineering and Technical Systems, National Research Council, evaluated the technologies that might be employed for the preservation of the paper records in the National Archives. The report concluded that, at the present time, microfilming technology is the least expensive and most effective technology for the preservation and access of documentary records.

During the same period that the above-cited report was being prepared, the Council on Library Resources, with funding from the Exxon Corporation, was examining technologies for the preservation of brittle books and other materials that were published on acidic paper from the 1860s to the present. While its Committee on Preservation and Access initially was enamored of the new technologies for image storage and retrieval, the Council, too, determined that microfilming technology is the most practical, cost-effective, and permanent method for the preservation and access of library and archival materials at this time. Microfilm is relatively inexpensive to produce, and its permanence, durability, and relative ease of use have been proven. It can readily be converted to another technology if that is desirable.

With further funding from Exxon, a group of research libraries established the first nonprofit regional center exclusively for preservation microfilming, the Mid-Atlantic Preservation Service (MAPS), located in Bethlehem, Pennsylvania. The founder and president of MAPS is C. Lee Jones, formerly with the Council on Library Resources. Jones has a firm grasp of the technical and managerial complexities in establishing and operating a nonprofit technical service, as well as a longstanding familiarity with the library and archival communities. NEH and other funding agencies, however, continue to support the preservation micro-filming activities at the first regional center established for library and archival materials: the Northeast Document Conservation Center (NEDCC) in Andover, Massachusetts. While it, too, can handle routine microfilming projects easily, NEDCC is able to deal with more fragile and difficult projects which would slow production at MAPS.

While there have been commercial microfilmers, such as University Microfilms, Research Publications, Chadwyck-Healey, and Clearwater, who have been willing to take on the microfilming of newspaper files that are commercially viable, a number of microfilming companies are now approaching libraries and archives with the promise of "preser-vation" services. With the considerable publicity about the newspaper and brittle book preservation microfilming projects, they no doubt envision the profits to be made from the efforts to preserve our documentary heritage. In addition, several commercial library binding companies that already provide an array of services to their customers are expanding to include preservation microfilming. While competition to meet library and archival needs is more than a little welcome, preservationists need to be assured that the quality of the work meets the standards necessary to ensure the permanence, durability, and accuracy of the filmed record.

The American Library Association publishes an important manual, *Preservation Microfilming* (Gwinn, 1987) that includes chapters on every aspect of preservation microfilming written by experts such as Sherry Byrne (University of Chicago) and Carolyn Harris (Columbia University), who have been involved with major preservation microfilming projects for a long time. While the manual does not focus on the particular problems surrounding the filming of newspapers, it is important that the people who are, and will be, involved in developing and implementing the state newspaper projects be familiar with its contents. Like any publication on a timely topic, the manual is already in need of modest revision, but its advice and recommendations can help avoid hours of work and costly errors.

It is critical that preservation microfilming be done correctly the first time around; there is rarely a second chance. Many newspaper files are too brittle to refilm. The task begins when newspapers are selected for filming. The keys to a successful program are bibliographic control and preparation prior to filming. Both of these aspects must be addressed before materials are sent to be filmed, and they are often the most costly part of a preservation microfilming project. To begin, it is essential to ensure that the newspaper, or a portion thereof, has not previously been filmed; conversely, it is essential to ensure that previous filming is adequate. All film must be carefully inspected.

The physical preparation of the newspaper for filming should, if at all possible, be done in-house. It is necessary to have trained professional staff to supervise the collation of the material to be filmed and the creation of the targets. Specifically, the supervisor of the project should have a degree in librarianship or the equivalent, bibliographical experience, and, if at all possible, previous microfilming experience. At the beginning, professional staff must decide a number of bibliographical matters, for example, whether each title change is to be cataloged and filmed separately, with a separate OCLC number and bibliographical notes to connect the files. For years, most newspaper files were filmed as they stood, and title changes were ignored. Although recording each title change and filming it separately is time-consuming, the procedure ensures bibliographical coherence and makes the newspaper more accessible to the user. The *Newspaper Cataloging Manual* recommends that each title change of a newspaper be recorded and filmed separately.

Each newspaper should be collated page-by-page. It is important to keep an accurate record of missing and badly damaged pages or other problems that could serve to confuse a reader. The table of contents for each reel of film needs to be programmed so that the filmers know beforehand what issues are to appear on a given reel. Targets that include the primary bibliographic information about the newspaper should be prepared. A target is a document or chart that contains identification information, coding or test charts. A target contains technical or bibliographic control information that is photographed on the film preceding or following the document. The preparation of targets can be accomplished with the help of a computer. Quality control is essential and is ultimately the responsibility of the repository. Each reel must be inspected for image quality and bibliographical accuracy.

A filmed newspaper file should not be disposed of until inspection is completed, no matter how substantial the file. (The New York Public Library had to hold one file for five months before filming and inspection were completed.)

There are a number of standards and specifications for the filming of newspapers; those who are responsible for the collections need to be thoroughly familiar with them before a project is undertaken. Standards protect the consumer by spelling out procedures. The standards and specifications that have been produced by the American National Standards Institute (ANSI), the Library of Congress, and other concerned bodies have evolved over time after experience with the microfilming medium. Developed by experts, the purpose of the standard is to aid and protect the consumer. A listing of standards is found in the appendix to *Preservation Microfilming* (Gwinn, 1987, pp. 175-177). They are followed by a sample preservation microfilming contract (pp. 178-187). The newspapers that are to be preserved in microformat should be filmed properly so that they will remain a permanent historical record. There has been some discussion about the filming of newspapers in microfiche. While this format has its advantages for storage and retrieval, few standards for fiche now exist. Thus, 35mm reel microfilm remains the medium for preservation.

First, a master negative is produced which is of archival quality (American National Standards Institute, 1984). The master negatives must be stored in a safe and secure vault; such vaults are located in several areas of the United States. Frequently, a printing master is also produced which can be used to make copies of the newspaper for general use, sale, or loan. It, too, should be stored under sound and secure conditions, separate from the service copies. The regional centers, Mid-Atlantic Preservation Service and the Northeast Document Conservation Center, will store printing masters for their customers. Both master negatives and printing masters need to be stored under environmentally sound conditions, with temperature and humidity controls and protection from fire, flood, or other catastrophe.

CONCLUSION

During the 1990s, the National Endowment for the Humanities and the Commission on Preservation and Access will direct considerable money and energy to ensure that materials of permanent value, published on impermanent paper, will be preserved. While the Commission's primary concern is with the microfilming of brittle books in U.S. libraries research collections, its efforts have made millions of people aware of the need to preserve the nation's documentary heritage. The preservation of newspapers has been recognized as one of the nation's priorities, with considerable support for the effort coming from the national government. But this is an effort that involves every state and nearly every community in the United States. It is an effort jointly undertaken by librarians, archivists, historians, the newspaper publishers themselves, as well as others in the community who care about the preservation of a national documentary heritage. And the effort is not limited by national boundaries; the libraries in this country, both great and small, contain files of newspapers that have come from every country in the world, newspapers which reflect their own national heritage. There are few libraries in the country that will not be involved on the local and state level in the United States Newspaper Program. It is an important effort, a part of the worldwide effort to preserve the newspaper—that everyday object that reflects our national character and the public events of everyday life.

ACKNOWLEDGEMENTS

The author wishes to thank the individuals who took the time to read the various drafts of this paper, make suggestions and corrections, and provide considerable detail about various aspects of the U.S. Newspaper Program and the bibliographic control and microfilming of newspapers. They include: Ronald Becker, Special Collections and Archives, Rutgers University Libraries; Timothy S. Corlis, Educational Testing Service (ETS), formerly with the New Jersey Newspaper Project; Jeffrey Field, Preservation Program Office, National Endowment for the Humanities; Robert Harriman, Technical Coordinator, U.S. Newspaper Project, Library of Congress; C. Lee Jones, President, Mid-Atlantic Preservation Service; Daniel Jones, New Jersey Bureau of Archives and Records Management; Karl Niederer, Director, Archives and Records Division, New Jersey Bureau of Archives and Records Management; Lorraine Perrotta, Getty Museum and Library, former head of the New York Public Library Newspaper Project; Lida Sak, Project Director, New Jersey Newspaper Project; and Paul Stellhorn, Newark (NJ) Public Library. The author is also grateful to Dr. David W. G. Clements, former Chief of the Preservation Division, British Library, for enlightening discussions about a technique for the strenghening of paper that is being developed at the University of Manchester, England.

REFERENCES

American National Standards Institute. (1984). *American national standard for photography (film)—Archival records, silver-gelatin type, or polyester base.* ANSI/ASC PH1.41-4. Washington, DC: ANSI.

Corlis, T. S., & Brown, J. (1988). USNP conference. *Conservation Administration News, 35* (October), 13.

Cunha, G. (1987). Mass deacidification. *Library Technology Reports, 23* (3), 361-472.

Cunha, G. (1989). Mass deacidification for Libraries: Update 1989. *Library Technology Reports, 25*(1), 5-82.

Field, J. (1986). The U. S. Newspaper Program. *Conservation Administration News, 25* (April), 5.

Field, J. (1988). The United States Newspaper Program. *British Library Newspaper Library Newsletter, 9* (January), 8.

Gregory, W. (1937 *American newspapers, 1821-1936: A union list of files available in the United States and Canada.* New York: H. W. Wilson.

Gwinn, N. E. (Ed.). (1987). *Preservation microfilming: A guide for librarians and archivists.* Chicago: American Library Association.

Hamilton, D. (1988). Keynote address. In I. P. Gibb (Ed.), *Newspaper preservation and access* (Vol. 1) (Proceedings of the Symposium held in London, 12-15 August 1987) (pp. 13-19). München: K. G. Saury.

Harriman, R. (1984). *Newspaper cataloguing manual.* Washington, DC: Library of Congress.

Hill, F. P. (1910). The deterioration of newspaper paper. *Library Journal, 35*(July), 299-301.

Jacobus, A. (1948). Binding in a newspaper library. *Special Libraries, 31*(July/August), 295.

McMaster, J. B. (1892). *A history of the people of the A United States: From the Revolution to the Civil War (Vos. 1-2).* New York: D. Appleton.

Mills, T. F. (1981). Preserving yesterday's news for today's historian: A brief history of newspaper preservation, bibliography and indexing. *Journal of Library History, 16*(3), 463-487.

A model for newspaper bibliographic projects: The final report of the Iowa Pilot Project of the United States Newspaper Project. (1978). Iowa City, IA and Washington, DC: State Historical Society of Iowa.

Scribner, B. W. (1934). *Preservation of newspaper records.* Washington, DC: National Bureau of Standards.

Smith, M., & Merrill-Oldham, J. (Eds.). (1985). *Library preservation program: Models, priorities, possibilities.* Chicago: American Library Association.

Sullivan, L. E. (1986). United States Newspaper Program: Progress and prospects. *Microform Review, 15*(3), 159-160.

U.S. Congress Office of Technology Assessment. (1988). *Book preservation technologies.* Washington, DC: USGPO.

Woods, E. W. (1988). Newspapers—Toward preserving a national resource. In L. N. Upham (Ed.), *Newspapers in the library* (pp. 4-5). New York: Haworth Press.

ANNOTATED BIBLIOGRAPHY

Bourke, T. A. (1986). The microfilming of newspapers: An overview. *Microform Review, 15*(3), 154-157.
   A history of the filming of newspapers at the New York Public Library with a brief report on current projects and filming methods.

Calmes, A. (1986). New confidence in microfilm. *Library Journal, 111*(15), 38-42.
   Reviews the advances in image reproduction technology during the past decade, comparing microfilm to optical disk as a preservation medium. A clear discussion of the advantages of microfilm over other copying technologies.

Carter, R. (Ed.). (1986). *The United States Newspaper Program: Cataloguing aspects.* New York: Haworth Press.

An issue of *Cataloguing and Classification Journal, 6*(4), that provides an overview of the bibliographic part of the program.

Field, J. (1985). The role of the National Endowment for the Humanities Office of Preservation in the national preservation effort. *Microform Review, 14*(2), 81-86.

Discusses the types of preservation projects that the office expects to support, with emphasis on cooperative projects set within a national context.

Field, J. (1987). The U.S. Newspaper Program. *Conservation Administration News, 30*(July, 5, 24.

Describes the goals and objectives of the program.

Frieder, R. (1987). The microfiche revolution in libraries. *Microform Review, 16*(3), 214-216.

Discusses the advantages and disadvantages of microfiche in library preservation; disadvantages include a lack of standards for preservation microfiche.

Harriman, R. (1985). *Newspaper cataloguing manual.* CONSER/USNP Edition. Washington, DC: Library of Congress.

The manual for the U.S. Newspaper Program's bibliographic work.

Harvey, R. (1988). Nothing left to access? The problem of deteriorating newspapers. *Education for librarianship: Australia, 5*(1), 18-26.

A discussion of the problems faced in Australia and the need for a national newspaper preservation plan. It is urged that preservation be included in the library school curriculum to ensure that librarians are trained to deal with the problems of preservation and access.

Holley, R. P. (1987). The Utah Newspaper Project. *Library Resources and Technical Services, 31*(2) , 177-191.

A detailed description of one state's project.

Library of Congress. (1972). *Specifications for the microfilming of newspapers in the Library of Congress.* Washington, DC: USGPO.

Preservation of historical records. (1986). Washington, DC: National Academy Press.

Various methods for preserving paper records are examined and alternative actions for preserving original documents or retaining more permanently the information contained in them are assessed.

Scribner, B.W. (1934). *Preservation of newspaper records.* Washington, DC: National Bureau of Standards (NBS Miscellaneous Publication 145).

The results of a survey of the paper used in newspapers published between 1830 and 1900 with suggestions for the production and preservation of newspapers.

Starr, M. J. (1986). The preservation of Canadian newspapers. *Microform Review, 15*(3), 162-164.

Describes the National Library of Canada's decentralized program for the preservation of Canadian newspapers.

Sullivan, L. E. (1986). United States Newspaper Program: Progress and prospects. *Microform Review, 15*(3), 158-161.

A brief history of newspaper publishing in the United States; a discussion of the factors leading to the U.S. Newspaper Program, its present situation, and its future.

Swartzell, A. (1988). Preservation microfilming: In-house initiated microforms. *Conservation Administration News, 34*(July), 6-7.

How to organize and implement a preservation microfilming program.

Upham, L. N. (Ed.). (1988). *Newspapers in the library: New approaches to management and reference work.* New York: Haworth Press. Monographic supplement #4 to *The Serials Librarian, 14,* 1988.

Papers on newspaper librarianship, with reference to the U.S. Newspaper Program and its effect on newspaper collections.

KLAUS B. HENDRIKS

Director, Conservation Research Division
National Archives of Canada
Ottawa, Ontario, Canada

The Preservation, Storage, and Handling of Black-and-White Photographic Records

INTRODUCTION

The English physician Richard Leach Maddox is generally credited with the invention of the silver gelatin glass plate negative. In 1871, he reported some experiments in which he used silver bromide salt, a light-sensitive compound, suspended in a gelatin layer to produce a negative picture after exposure in a camera (Maddox, 1871). The purpose of his experiments was to find a replacement for the liquid collodion which was used at the time as a binding agent for making glass plate negatives. This wet collodion process had the much-lamented disadvantage that the glass plates had to be exposed right after coating lest they lose their sensitivity to light. While the experiments performed by Maddox did not lead to any marketable product, let alone to a photographic material resembling anything on the market today, they did incite other experimentally minded photographers to continue using gelatin as a binding agent, until the Liverpool Dry Plate Company in 1878 placed the first silver gelatin dry plate negatives on the market under the name Bennett Dry Plates. The term *dry plates* was used to distinguish the gelatin materials from the collodion wet plates with their limitations, as noted above. The experiments performed by Maddox ushered in *the era of silver gelatin photographic technology*. The new materials had a number of advantages over all previous methods of producing photographs. For example, the glass plates could be manufactured by machines and so obtained a consistent quality. A second advantage was that the finished plate was light sensitive, i.e., it did not have to be sensitized immediately before exposure in a camera. Third, the coated, light-sensitive plates, i.e., the raw stock, kept their sensitivity for weeks and months, which allowed them to be shipped and stored before being sold. Most important, manufacturers learned how to control precisely the properties of the final product and to adjust these properties to an intended purpose.

Consequently, numerous types of negative materials have now appeared on the market, all tailored to specific applications. Silver gelatin photographic technology has dominated photography for approximately the past one hundred years. It has produced diverse products such as negative films for studio work, duplication and copying work, motion pictures, microfilming, x-ray films, astronomical photography, aerial photography, and others.

Processed silver gelatin films and papers contain finely divided particles of silver distributed throughout a gelatin layer which has a thickness of about 0.01 mm. According to strict physical terminology, the silver particles form a suspension in the gelatin, but traditionally the term *emulsion* has been used to describe the image layer.

FACTORS AFFECTING STABILITY OF PHOTOGRAPHIC IMAGES

The subject of this article is the preservation of processed black-and-white photographic records in libraries. Since silver gelatin photographic films and papers have been around for about a century, and since by far the largest number of black-and-white photographic images are silver gelatin images, knowledge of the properties of these records is extensive. Factors that may affect their stability are, for the most part, well known. They are listed in general form in Table 1 in order of decreasing importance.

TABLE 1
FACTORS AFFECTING THE PERMANENCE OF
BLACK-AND-WHITE PHOTOGRAPHIC MATERIALS

Relative humidity
Oxidizing chemicals
Temperature
Light
Handling and use

Relative Humidity

Relative humidity constitutes the overriding influence in the permanence of photographs. Moisture catalyzes or accelerates many chemical reactions, and some mechanisms of image degradation in black-and-white photographs simply would not occur in a dry environment. One example is the reaction of residual processing chemicals with silver particles in a photographic image to produce discoloration; this deterioration does not occur in a completely dry environment. Another relates to acidity. It has been observed that the presence of moisture is necessary to produce acidic conditions in paper that contains certain chemical compounds. Since the concept of acidity applies only to (generally aqueous) solutions, water — in whatever form — must be present to produce an acidic reaction. Known examples of compounds that can produce acidity in the presence of moisture are alum rosin size, as an internal source, and sulfur dioxide, which may be absorbed into the paper from the surrounding atmosphere. A third example of the effect of relative humidity relates to the physical changes that can occur to objects when relative humidity changes. Some materials expand in an environment of high humidity and contract if that condition is reversed. This is demonstrated impressively by archival records that have a layer structure of two components which react differently to changing relative humidity.

Photographic records are a case in point. The gelatin layer that carries the image has a high affinity for water, which it absorbs quickly when available. Conversely, in dry conditions, the gelatin layer dries out faster than the support — either plastic film or paper — and contracts at a rate that forces the photograph to curl up. A change to high humidity will quickly relax and flatten such a photograph. Thus, relative humidity is well established to be the overriding single factor controlling the longevity of photographs.

Oxidizing Chemicals, Temperature, and Light

A truly devastating effect might be expected by the action of a combination of any two conditions listed in Table 1. This is true in particular if one of these conditions is the presence of oxidizing chemicals. While well-processed contemporary black-and-white photographic records are essentially stable with regard to heat and light, the image-forming substance — elemental silver, as noted — is sensitive to chemical oxidation reactions triggered by aggressive chemical compounds capable of reacting with the image silver.

Examples of materials that have been observed to cause discoloration to black-and-white photographs include adhesives from the seam used in filing enclosures; deposits from fingerprints; inscriptions in ink on silver gelatin glass plate negatives; and chemicals emanating from newsprint, which cause a noticeable effect after photographic negatives are kept for some time in close contact with newspaper clippings. The exact nature of the compounds causing these discolorations is not known. However, several cases of deterioration of image silver have been well documented in the technical literature, with corresponding identification of the nature of the aggressive compounds. Table 2 gives some examples of degradation reactions which have been confirmed by laboratory experiments, along with the corresponding references.

The technique of attempting to recreate a deterioration reaction in the laboratory is worth explaining. To begin with an analogy, in the chemistry of natural products it has been customary for decades to isolate in pure form a specific compound whose existence is somehow suspected—for example, an antibiotic—and to determine its often complex molecular structure. After all physical and chemical properties of the new compound, including its geometrical structure, have been determined, chemists attempt the crowning achievement, which is to synthesize the natural product in the laboratory. If all the properties of

TABLE 2

KNOWN SOURCES OF CHEMICALS THAT CONTRIBUTE
TO THE DEGRADATION OF SILVER IMAGES

Source	*Active Chemical Compound*	*Reference*
Cellulose nitrate (decomposing)	Nitrogen oxides	Carroll and Calhoun, 1955
Aging cardboard containers	Peroxides	Henn and Wiest, 1963
Electrostatic copy machines	Ozone	Weyde, 1969
Car exhaust gases	Nitrogen oxides; sulfur oxides	Weyde, 1972
Oil based paints	Peroxides	Feldman, 1981
Residual processing chemicals	Thiosulfate and its complexes	Numerous; cf. Eaton, 1970; Kopperl and Huttemann, 1986
Adhesives used in mounting print	Thiourea	Hendirks, 1989
Laboratory tests	Neutral and acid peroxides; sulfides; cumene peroxide; zinc dust; peroxide plus sulfide	Henn and Mack, 1965

the synthetic product are identical with the compound isolated from nature, then, and only then, can the structure of the new compound be said to be confirmed. Similarly, if a characteristic type of deterioration has occurred to a photograph in its natural environment, it is possible to speculate on a possible cause in order to confirm that cause in laboratory experiments.

A specific example may illustrate this. Some photographic prints made during the first decade of photography and mounted on album pages show pronounced fading along the four edges of the picture. A likely cause for that discoloration is the adhesive that was used to attach the photograph to the mountboard. These early photographic prints are of a type known as salted paper prints. Sample photographs can be prepared by that process in the laboratory today in order to study the effect of various kinds of adhesives, applied to the back of photographs, on the stability of the image silver. Adhesives used in the nineteenth-century were largely either of animal origin, generally called glues, or derived from plants, when they are referred to as pastes. After application of numerous commercially available glues and pastes to sample prints made for the purpose, it was established in the author's laboratory that pastes show no harmful effects on salted paper prints. By contrast, animal glue did cause discoloration of the image silver under accelerated aging conditions, as well as in normal room conditions, where the reaction takes a little more time to occur. Glue—a coarse and unrefined material related to gelatin—was chemically analyzed by a complicated process known as amino acid analysis which revealed the presence of at least one compound that is capable of reacting with image silver even in high dilution. The compound is called *thiourea*. When applied in various concentrations to the back of photographic prints, it is capable of migrating through the paper base and reacting with the image silver to cause discoloration (Hendriks, 1989).

Turning back to Table 2, it may be seen that the effect of residual processing chemicals, in particular fixing salts, is among the most thoroughly studied reasons for image silver degradation (Eaton, 1970). Discovered within the first two decades of photography, it remains an important subject of studies and experimental work today (Kopperl & Huttemann, 1986). Of special interest to librarians is the occurrence of redox blemishes on processed microfilms. The term *redox* is an abbre-viation for reduction-oxidation and indicates the chemical mechanism by which the blemishes are formed. Another term often used to describe them is *microspots*. Redox blemishes are generally too small to be seen with the naked eye, but a glance through an ordinary light microscope at a magnification of 50X or higher will easily reveal their presence. They usually occur on negative films, i.e., camera original microfilm, that have been stored in cardboard boxes. Such boxes, if they contain groundwood, can emit peroxide. *Peroxides* are gaseous compounds which can be envisaged as reactive forms of oxygen and are capable of chemically attacking image silver in processed microfilm. The result is the formation of redox blemishes: microscopically small, circular spots of an orange-red color (Henn & Wiest, 1963). The blemishes are not contagious. If the source of the oxidizing chemicals is removed, formation of redox blemishes ceases. In practice, it is recommended that processed microfilm rolls be removed from cardboard boxes and be stored in either metal cases or in boxes of rigid polypropylene which are supplied by photographic manufacturers.

The danger posed by the presence of peroxides and similar, chemically active compounds has been confirmed by studies on other materials that were observed to have detrimental effects on black-and-white photographs. For example, it was reported in 1981 that freshly applied oil-based paints produce peroxides during drying, which can affect photographs kept in recently painted rooms (Feldman, 1981). While J. F. Carroll and John M. Calhoun (1955) described in detail the effect of gaseous nitrogen oxides emanating from aging cellulose nitrate films, R. W. Henn and B. D. Mack (1965) published experimental conditions for the artificial aging of silver gelatin microfilms through exposure to various oxidizing atmospheres under laboratory conditions. Other examples of potential danger include the presence of ozone produced in the vicinity of electrostatic copy machines (Weyde, 1969), certain compounds present in automobile exhaust gases (Weyde, 1972), and as described earlier, sulfur-containing substances that are part of animal glues. All these conditions which have been observed in actual conditions of storage and use have been replicated in laboratory experiments.

Handling and Use

Along with the potentially harmful effects of a combination of oxidizing chemicals with either high relative humidity or temperature, ranks the influence of handling and use on the well-being of photographs. Photographic materials are in high demand in their numerous applications: for study and research, publications, and exhibitions. Widespread handling can present a danger to rare historical photographs. Microfilm, so widely used as a preservation medium, suffers mechanical damage from frequent consultation by microfilm readers. Fortunately, the clients' copies are positive images which can be reprinted from the original camera negative. The purpose of these negative originals, in some institutions referred to as master copies of valuable historical documents, is to make positive user copies. The camera originals can be placed into inactive storage for many years without concern for their stability. They are taken out only for the purpose of making additional positive prints when the previous set has been worn out. The historical document itself need never be used in its original form.

Correct handling of still photographic images is, for the most part, a matter of common sense. Since negatives and prints are liable to be damaged physically through fingerprints or scratches, unsleeved negatives and prints should be handled only by people wearing protective gloves made of lintless cotton or nylon. This is general practice in major photographic collections. Ideally, photographs are handled in a clean, dust-free environment. No food or drinks should be tolerated in their vicinity. Photographs should not be left lying around unattended or unprotected. Exposure to direct sunlight will result in lasting damage to any photographic image. Large-format negatives or prints must neither be rolled nor folded. Care must be taken not to damage the corners and edges of a photographic print while examining it. This can largely be prevented if prints are mounted before handling them. Paper prints should not be stapled or attached to other documents with paper clips. Inscriptions in common ink are liable to fade when photographs are on display and will invariably bleed or become illegible if accidentally immersed in water. This is not likely to happen if special inks are used which are manufactured for the purpose of marking prints permanently. Examples of pens with permanent inks are Lumocolor 313 by Staedtler and Film/Printing Marking Pen available from Light Impressions in Rochester, New York. If something must be written on the back of photographic prints to identify them, a soft lead pencil is the preferred medium. Inscriptions in pencil will neither smear nor bleed or transfer when immersed in water, but remain erasable should it become necessary to change the inscription (Hendriks & Dobrusskin, 1990). For optimum protection, negatives and prints should be placed first into sleeves of uncoated polyester or cellulose triacetate (both commercially available), and then in paper envelopes on which is written all necessary documentation. Prints can be viewed without removing them from the transparent sleeve.

A further consideration regarding the preservation of documentary or artistic still photographic prints is the effect of display upon their stability. The use of photographic pictures in exhibitions is becoming increasingly common. Such use requires that photographs be matted and mounted, framed, packed into boxes or crates, shipped by various means, unpacked, hung onto walls, exposed to changing environmental conditions, etc. Photographs must also be taken down after the exhibition and shipped back to their home base. Keepers of photograph collections are well-advised to consider the implications of photographs on display and to prepare thoroughly and well the arrangements for an exhibition in order to avoid disappointment later.

Table 3 summarizes some principal strategies for preventing photographic materials from being damaged.

ENVIRONMENTAL STORAGE CONDITIONS

It is ironic that the recommendations for the storage of processed photographic materials written by the American National Standards Institute (ANSI) do not contain maximum permissible threshold values for concentrations of oxidizing gases in storage areas. An excellent example to follow would be the clean-room conditions set by photographic manufacturers. These spaces must be dark for obvious reasons and completely free of dust, particulate matter, and gases such as hydrogen sulfide, sulfur dioxide, and hydrogen peroxide. Some manufacturers have not instituted specific numerical values for clean-room conditions. The purification of the atmosphere in the manufacturing areas is so effective that the concentrations of any of the above irritants are beyond the ability of analytical techniques to detect them. That is, any present air pollution is below the detection limit of modern analytical instruments!

Temperature and Relative Humidity Levels

Current ANSI standards regarding the storage of processed photographic materials address mainly temperature and relative humidity levels. Table 4 summarizes recommendations for the storage of photographic plates (ANSI, 1981).

Recommendations are set at realistic levels. The wide temperature range within which photographic plates can be kept indicates the slight effect that temperature alone is expected to have on their stability. While a relative humidity of below 40 percent is preferable, any level

TABLE 3
PRESERVATION: PREVENTIVE MEASURES

1. Provision of correct storage conditions
2. Use of correct storage enclosures [sleeves; envelopes; boxes; cans]
3. Instructions for handling and use
4. Instructions concerning display conditions
5. Provision of emergency plans
6. Application of copying and duplication techniques

TABLE 4
ANSI PH1.45-1981
PRACTICE FOR STORAGE OF PROCESSED PHOTOGRAPHIC PLATES

	Storage Temperature	*Relative Humidity*
Recommended:	15-25°C. (59-77°F.)	20-50%
Preferably:	20°C. (68°F.)	40%

between 20 and 50 percent is acceptable. Table 5 shows similar recommendations for the storage of photographic paper prints (ANSI, 1987).

Recommended environmental conditions are similar to those for photographic plates. The maximum permissible threshold value of 60 percent relative humidity is significant. A high moisture content of the air is conducive to mold growth, which can completely destroy the image in time. Daily cycling of more than 4°C should also be avoided. Specifications for the storage of processed photographic film are divided into one set for medium-term and another for archival. *Medium-term film* is a photographic film that is suitable for the preservation of records for a minimum of ten years. *Archival film* is a photographic film suitable for the preservation of records having permanent historical value. Table 6 summarizes the recommended relative humidity and temperature conditions for the storage of processed photographic film for *medium-term* storage (ANSI, 1985). Film includes all the variations mentioned earlier.

Table 7 shows the recommended relative humidity and temperature conditions for the storage of processed photographic film for *archival* storage.

Table 7 features a confusing range of recommended relative humidity levels. Upon closer examination, it becomes clearer that the materials listed in the extreme left column of Table 7 can be rearranged so as to group together films of similar composition with respect to the support and the nature of the image-bearing layer. There are three such support groups: conventionally processed silver or dye (color) gelatin images on a cellulose ester base; silver or dye (color) gelatin images on a polyester base; and nonsilver, nongelatin images on either base.

Regrouped together in this fashion, the recommendations for relative humidity are shown in Table 8. In the new arrangement, materials of similar properties with regard to their reactivity towards

TABLE 5
ANSI PH1.48-1982 (R1987)
AMERICAN NATIONAL STANDARD FOR PHOTOGRAPHS (FILMS AND
SLIDES)—BLACK-AND-WHITE PHOTOGRAPHIC PAPER PRINTS—
PRACTICE FOR STORAGE

	Storage Temperature	*Relative Humidity*
Acceptable:	15-25°C. (59-77°F.)	30-50%
Never:	30°C. (86°F.) Avoid daily cycling of 4°C. (7°F.)	60%

changing relative humidity levels are combined because they require similar RH levels for long-term permanence. For example, gelatin layers and cellulose acetate bases behave similarly with regard to their shrinking properties; by contrast, gelatin contracts at a faster rate than polyester at low RH; consequently, 30 percent is the minimum recommendation for that system. In addition, polyester may become too brittle below that value. Since materials in the third group do not contain gelatin layers, interactions do not occur between support and binding mediums due to their different shrinkage characteristics. Finally, color photographic films have the narrowest recommended RH range, of which the higher threshold value (30 percent) is in the interest of the permanence of the dyes, whereas the lower level (25 percent) is designated for the benefit of the polyester support.

Since few photographic collections could afford several storage areas with different RH levels for various materials, the new arrangement, most importantly, facilitates the selection of a single optimum RH level beneficial to a variety of photographic films. That level should be 30 percent, plus or minus three percent, in line with the most recent recommendations for the storage of paper records in archives and libraries, and significantly lower than the 50 percent RH recommended a decade ago for the storage of such materials.

Natural Disaster Contingency Plans

Stored photographic materials are threatened by floods, fire, and the aftereffects of attempts to extinguish a fire. Contingency plans for dealing with natural disasters are therefore necessary in archives and libraries, and should include provisions for photograph collections. A recent publication from the author's laboratory summarized the results

TABLE 6

ANSI PH1.43-1985

AMERICAN NATIONAL STANDARD FOR PHOTOGRAPHY (FILM)

PROCESSED SAFETY FILM — STORAGE

RECOMMENDED RELATIVE HUMIDITY AND TEMPERATURE

CONDITIONS FOR MEDIUM-TERM STORAGE

Sensitive Layer	*Base Type*	*Relative Humidity Range (%)*	*Maximum Temperature (°C.)*
Microfilm:			
Silver-gelatin	Cellulose ester	15-60	25
Silver-gelatin	Polyester	30-60	25
Heat-processed silver	Polyester	15-60	25
General:			
Silver-gelatin	Cellulose ester	15-60	25
Silver-gelatin	Polyester	30-60	25
Color	Cellulose ester	15-30	10
Color	Polyester	25-30	10
Diazo	Cellulose ester	15-50	25
Diazo	Polyester	15-50	25
Vesicular	Polyester	15-60	25
Electrophotographic	Polyester	15-60	25
Photoplastic	Polyester	15-60	25

of an extensive study on the recovery of water-soaked photographic materials (Hendriks & Lesser, 1983). Ideally, water-soaked photographs are air-dried. This should be done if enough space is available to spread out the water-soaked photographic records. Time is also required for air drying. However, the significant result of the study was the observation that most photographic materials, including all contemporary silver gelatin and dye gelatin photographs, can be frozen after they have been soaked in water and can be left in the frozen state for some time to await later treatment. Freezing slows down dramatically any further degradation and so provides time for gradual recovery. Frozen photographs should be thawed and air-dried which is the preferred second option after air drying without freezing. A third possibility is freeze-drying photographs in a vacuum chamber, which leaves photographs virtually unharmed. Freeze-drying means that the photographs are kept during this process below 0°C, i.e., in the frozen state. By contrast, freezing followed by thawing and vacuum-drying at 4°C, i.e., above the freezing point of water — as is done with books — is not recommended because of blocking or sticking of gelatin layers. When wet, gelatin has adhesive properties which cause photographic negatives or prints packed in a bundle to stick together. It must be emphasized

TABLE 7
ANSI PH1.43-1985
AMERICAN NATIONAL STANDARD FOR PHOTOGRAPHY (FILM)
PROCESSED SAFETY FILM—STORAGE
RECOMMENDED RELATIVE HUMIDITY AND TEMPERATURE
CONDITIONS FOR ARCHIVAL STORAGE

Sensitive Layer	Base Type	Relative Humidity Range (%)	Maximum Temperature (°C.)
Microfilm:			
Silver-gelatin	Cellulose ester	15-40	21
Silver-gelatin	Polyester	30-40	21
Heat-processed silver	Polyester	15-50	21
General:			
Silver-gelatin	Cellulose ester	15-50	21
Silver-gelatin	Polyester	30-50	21
Color	Cellulose ester	15-30	2
Color	Polyester	25-30	2
Diazo	Cellulose ester	15-30	21
Diazo	Polyester	15-30	21
Vesicular	Polyester	15-50	21
Electrophotographic	Polyester	15-50	21
Photoplastic	Polyester	15-50	21

that glass plates made by the wet collodion process, including the collodion positives known as ambrotypes and tintypes, are the materials which are most susceptible to water damage. They should neither be frozen nor freeze-dried once they have been immersed in water. Other exceptions to the recommendations given above are daguerreotypes and color lantern slides made by the pre-1935 additive color processes (such as Lumiere Autochrome Transparency Plates, Agfacolor Plates, and others). Samples of these photographs were not included in the experiments on disaster recovery.

CONCLUSION

Conventional silver halide photography is being replaced in many applications by electronic imaging technologies, particularly by video imaging. Cost effectiveness and the instant availability of the image on a viewing screen are but two reasons for this change. Traditional photographic materials have one particular requirement that seems to be dreaded by anyone involved in photography: they are the only materials collected in archives and libraries that require processing in

TABLE 8
ANSI PH1.43-1985
AMERICAN NATIONAL STANDARD FOR PHOTOGRAPHY (FILM)
PROCESSED SAFETY FILM—STORAGE
OPTIMUM STORAGE RELATIVE HUMIDITY FOR ARCHIVAL STORAGE

Sensitive Layer	*Base Type*	*Relative Humidity Range (%)*
1. Cellulose Acetate/Gelatin/Silver or Dye:		
Silver-gelatin (Microfilm)	Cellulose ester	15-40
Silver-gelatin	Cellulose ester	15-60
Color	Cellulose ester	15-50
2. Polyester/Gelatin/Silver or Dye		
Silver-gelatin	Polyester	30-40
Silver-gelatin	Polyester	30-50
Color	Polyester	25-30
3. Polyester or Cellulose Ester/Nongelatin/ Nonsilver		
Diazo	Cellulose ester	15-30
Diazo	Polyester	15-30
Vesicular	Polyester	15-50
Electrophotographic	Polyester	15-50
Photoplastic	Polyester	15-50
Heat-Processed Silver	Polyester	15-50

a series of chemical solutions in order to produce a visible record. From a technical point of view, processing can actually be used as an important tool to control or determine the properties of the final image, such as contrast, resolution, and graininess; but it is often not well-understood and is done preferably by machines which require little human intervention. Processing is also one of three factors that may have a profound effect on the permanence of the record, the other two being the inherent properties built in during the manufacture of the material and the conditions under which it is kept. The requirement for chemical processing of photographic records and its perceived uncertainties have contributed much to the declining popularity of chemical processing when compared with electronic imaging. It is worthwhile to remember, however, that modern black-and-white film bases used in the manufacture of microfilm, motion-picture film, aerial film, and still photographic negatives are made to such rigid specifications and have been tested so extensively that they merit their official recognition as permanent records materials. They remain the only nonpaper records in libraries and archives having that status. They are human-readable, and their permanence under a given set of conditions is well-established. Modern safety film is clearly superior to any other nonpaper, nonparchment record materials in common use or under consideration for use in libraries and archives.

REFERENCES

American National Standards Institute. (1982). American National Standard for Photography (Films and Slides). *Black-and-white photographic paper prints—Practice for storage.* ANSI PH1.48-1982 (R1987). New York: American National Standards Institute.

American National Standards Institute. (1981). *Practice for storage of processed photographic plates.* ANSI PH1.45-1981. New York: American National Standards Institute.

American National Standards Institute. (1985). American National Standard for Photography (Film). *Processed safety film—Storage.* ANSI PH1.43-1985. New York: American National Standards Institute.

Carroll, J. F., & Calhoun, J. M. (1955). Effect of nitrogen oxide gases on processed acetate film. *Journal of the Society of Motion Picture and Television Engineers, 64*(September), 501-507.

Eaton, G. (1970). Preservation, deterioration, restoration of photographic images. *Library Quarterly, 40*(1), 85-99.

Feldman, L. H. (1981). Discoloration of black-and-white photographic prints. *Journal of Applied Photographic Engineering, 7*(1), 1-9.

Hendriks, K. B. (1989). The stability and preservation of recorded images. In V. K. Walworth, J. M. Sturge & A. Shepp (Eds.), *Imaging processes and materials. Neblette's eighth Edition* (pp. 637-684). New York: Van Nostrand Reinhold.

Hendriks, K. B., & Dobrusskin, S. (1990). *Marking photographic prints.* Unpublished manuscript.

Hendriks, K. B., & Lesser, B. (1983). Disaster preparedness and recovery: Photographic materials. *American Archivist, 46*(1), 52-68.

Henn, R. W., & Mack, B. D. (1965). A gold protective treatment for microfilm. *Photographic Science and Engineering, 9*(6), 378-384.

Henn, R. W., & Wiest, D. G. (1963). Microscopic spots in processed microfilm: Their nature and prevention. *Photographic Science and Engineering, 7*(5), 253-261.

Kopperl, D. F., & Hutteman, T. J. (1986). Effect of residual thiosulfate ion on the image stability of microfilms. *Journal of Imaging Technology, 12*(4), 173-180.

Maddox, R. L. (1871). An experiment with gelatino-bromide. *British Journal of Photography, 18*(592), 422-423.

Weyde, E. (1972). A simple test to identify gases which destroy silver images. *Photographic Science and Engineering, 16*(4), 283-286.

Weyde, E. (1969). *Stabilitat von Silberbildern* [Stability of silver photographs]. *Chimia, 23*(1), 42-43.

HENRY WILHELM

Director of Research
Preservation Publishing Company
Grinnell, Iowa

Color Photographs and Color Motion Pictures in the Library: For Preservation or Destruction?

INTRODUCTION

Kodachrome, the first practical color film, was introduced in 1935. "Becky Sharp," the first full-color Technicolor feature film, was released the same year, and Kodacolor film, a color negative film for ordinary, fixed-exposure box cameras, was put on the market in 1942. Nonetheless, it took until about 1965 for the mass conversion from black-and-white to color photography to begin in earnest. Today, an overwhelming majority of photographs and motion pictures are made with color materials. In some branches of photography—portrait and wedding photography, for example—a black-and-white photograph is now almost unheard of.

With the change to color, however, a heavy price was paid. The images of most color photographs are composed of organic dyes that are inherently far less stable than the (potentially) long-lasting silver images of correctly processed black-and-white photographs. Color photographs fade when exposed to light, whereas the metallic silver images of black-and-white photographs are, in themselves, largely unaffected by light. Most types of color photographs gradually fade and stain even when kept in the dark; this can be prevented only by low-temperature, humidity-controlled storage.

Color Print Materials

Prints made on current Kodak Ektacolor papers and similar color negative print materials supplied by other manufacturers may exhibit objectionable fading, color shift, and/or yellowish stain in less than ten years under typical indoor display conditions. The rate of fading is more or less proportional to the intensity of illumination; prints displayed in a very bright area will fade much more rapidly than those exposed to lower levels of light. Some products last longer on display than others. Fujicolor Paper Super FA paper, introduced in 1990, is perhaps the most stable color negative print paper currently available. No color paper, however, is sufficiently stable to permit long-term display.

Since their introduction in 1942, color negative print papers traditionally have had poor dark-storage stability. In most cases this is manifested by progressive cyan dye loss (resulting in a color shift toward red) and yellowish stain formation, which is most apparent in the whites and lighter parts of the image. Not a single print from the first decade of Kodacolor is known to have survived in good condition; thus, this entire era of amateur color prints has been totally lost.

Beginning with the introduction of Konica Color Paper Type SR in 1984, the dye stability of color negative papers in dark storage has been significantly improved compared with that of earlier materials, but the prints still require refrigerated storage for long-term keeping. Corresponding improvements in light fading stability (and, in most cases, rates of yellowish stain formation in dark storage) have not yet been achieved.

Color Motion Pictures

The stability of color motion pictures, most of which are now made with a negative/positive color process that is in most key respects similar to that used with still-camera color negatives and prints, has, with some exceptions, been significantly improved in the last few years; however, color motion pictures continue to require low-temperature, humidity-controlled storage for long-term preservation. Most motion picture color negatives and prints made between the introduction of the Eastman Color process in 1950 and until about 1985 (when improved products were introduced) have by now suffered significant fading. Most Eastman Color prints made between 1950 and around 1970 have now lost nearly all of the cyan dye component of their images and usually much of the yellow dye as well, so all that remains is a ghastly reddish-magenta reminder of what once were brilliant, full-color images.

Color Slides

Color slides can fade rapidly when subjected to the intense illumination of a slide projector. Kodachrome film, for example, suffers a noticeable loss of magenta dye after only about twenty minutes of intermittent projection. The loss of image detail and the color shift toward green are especially noticeable in highlight portions of the image.

HUMIDITY-CONTROLLED COLD STORAGE
FOR LONG-TERM PRESERVATION

The stability shortcomings of color photographs present special problems in library collections. With the exception of post-1939 Kodachrome films that have been kept in the dark, most color photographs and non-Technicolor motion pictures made from 1935 until perhaps 1980 have by now suffered significant, even catastrophic, fading. To prevent further losses, librarians should identify important and/or irreplaceable color prints, slides, and motion pictures in their collections and make copies for use purposes; the originals must be placed in humidity-controlled cold storage. A temperature of 0°F (−18°C) or lower and a relative humidity of 30 percent are recommended.

Institutions currently operating cold storage facilities meeting these requirements include the John Fitzgerald Kennedy Library, Boston, Massachusetts (1979); the National Aeronautics and Space Administration (NASA), Houston, Texas (1982) and White Sands, New Mexico (1987); the Historic New Orleans Collection, New Orleans, Louisiana (1987); and the Biblioteca Nacional in Caracas, Venezuela (projected for 1991).

Estimates based on data from "Arrhenius-type" accelerated dark fading tests conducted by the major photographic manufacturers (including Eastman Kodak Company; Fuji Photo Film Co., Ltd.; Konica Corporation; and Agfa-Gevaert AG) indicate that, when stored at 0°F or lower with controlled relative humidity, color materials can be considered to be "permanent," with even the most unstable products probably lasting longer than 1,000 years before a 10 percent, or "just noticeable," dye loss occurs. Cold storage preserves not only the dye image but also the base material and gelatin emulsion as well. Kept at 0°F, color photographs can be expected to far outlast black-and-white photographs stored under normal room temperature conditions. An Arrhenius-type accelerated test is specified in the new IT9.9-1990 American National Standards Institute (ANSI) standard for test methods for measuring the stability of color photographic images.

Compared with storage at a more moderate temperature (e.g., 35°F), storage at 0°F offers a tremendous increase in the life of color materials and is well worth the small additional costs associated with constructing and operating a 0°F vault. Controlling the relative humidity in a cold storage vault is, in the long run, a more effective and less expensive storage method than sealing films and prints in vapor-proof containers and keeping them in a non- humidity-controlled vault.

Frost-free, home-type refrigerators have provided a low-cost cold storage option for institutions such as the Academy of Natural Sciences in Philadelphia, where the VIREO collection uses a number of these refrigerators in its well-managed collection of bird photographs. Institutions that temporarily are unable to provide cold storage for their collections can rent refrigerated space (38°F and 40 percent RH) by the cubic foot at moderate cost from the Records Center of Kansas City, a high-security underground storage facility located in Kansas City, Missouri.

The Peabody Museum of Archaeology and Ethnology at Harvard University has developed a compact, low-cost, slide-based visual reference system for color slides kept in its cold storage vault. The preservation program for original spaceflight color films at NASA is particularly noteworthy and can serve as a model for other institutions. The NASA program is especially applicable for institutions holding large collections of valuable color motion picture film.

Preservation of Cellulose Nitrate Film in Cold Storage

Because of the relatively poor stability of cellulose nitrate film and the fire hazards associated with the film, it has often been advised that all nitrate films be duplicated and the originals disposed of. However, nitrate still-camera negatives and motion picture negatives and prints (both black-and-white and color) that are still in good condition can be preserved almost indefinitely—perhaps more than 1,000 years—by placing them in humidity-controlled cold storage at 0°F (−18°C). John M. Calhoun (1953) of the Eastman Kodak Company explained:

> The rate of decomposition of cellulose nitrate is also very dependent on temperature and moisture content. The temperature coefficient of the reaction is about 4 per 10°C. or 2 per 10°F. which means that the rate of decomposition approximately doubles for every 10°F. increase in storage temperature. Moisture absorbed from the air, the amount of which is determined by the relative humidity, also accelerates the decomposition reaction. (p. 5)

Based on these figures, nitrate film should last about 32 times longer when stored at 25°F, and approximately *180 times longer* when stored at 0°F, than when the film is stored at 75°F. These figures are only estimates, but they do illustrate the dramatic increase in the life of nitrate films afforded by low-temperature, humidity-controlled storage. It seems clear that the common belief that nitrate films "cannot be preserved" is simply not correct. It further appears almost certain that nitrate films that are still in good condition when placed in 0°F storage will last much longer than conventionally processed duplicate negatives made on modern safety-base film kept under normal room-temperature conditions. Indeed, if Calhoun's estimates of the influence of temperature on the rate of decomposition are even remotely correct, low-temperature storage of nitrate film will preserve it for many hundreds of years—and possibly even for several thousand years. In this respect, the temperature coefficient of cellulose nitrate decomposition appears to be not unlike that of the fading of color photographs: both types of materials benefit greatly from low-temperature storage.

It is much less expensive to preserve original nitrate materials in low-temperature storage than it is to copy them onto modern safety film; in addition, image-quality losses are unavoidable in the copying process and it is always best to be able to go back to the original (or as close to the original as possible) when making use copies. With the availability of improved, electronic defect-suppression and image-enhancement techniques, access to original materials for making copies will become even more crucial in the future.

It is recommended that current nitrate duplication efforts be halted. Instead, a nationwide effort should be launched to construct a large-scale, safe, humidity-controlled 0°F (or lower) cold storage facility to preserve all of the cellulose nitrate motion film and still-camera negatives that still remain in collections. This project should proceed with the utmost urgency and should enlist the support of museums and archives, federal and state governments, and the entertainment film industry. With the films safely in low-temperature storage—and steady deterioration and continuing loss of the films halted—production of copies for projection and study purposes can proceed on a more timely basis.

Even when nitrate films have already been copied for preservation purposes, the originals should never be discarded unless they have reached an advanced stage of deterioration. It is particularly important that original Technicolor prints made on nitrate film be preserved in the best possible condition. (They should never be projected.)

DISPLAY OF COLOR PRINTS

For display of color prints, 300 Lux (28 fc) glass-filtered tungsten illumination is recommended; lower light levels, while slowing the rate of fading, generally are inadequate for proper visual appreciation of color images. (The length of time that original color prints can be displayed safely will, in any event, be limited.)

When most types of color prints are displayed, visible light—not ultraviolet radiation—is the primary cause of image fading. Most modern color print materials are made with UV-absorbing emulsion layers and, therefore, framing the prints with Plexiglas UF-3 or other UV filter (or placing a UV filter over the light source) generally affords little if any improvement in light fading stability.

Facsimile copy prints should be employed for routine display and reference. (Ilford Cibachrome materials used with Cibachrome camera/processors are recommended for this purpose.) When original color prints or other types of unstable photographs, such as albumen prints, are to be displayed, the photographs should be monitored with an electronic densitometer, and fading and/or staining levels should not be permitted to exceed predetermined limits (Wilhelm, 1981). The Art Institute of Chicago has implemented such a monitoring program for sensitive materials in its collection (Severson, 1986, 1987).

CONCLUSION

Libraries and other collecting institutions should keep up to date on the stability characteristics of available color print and film materials (Wilhelm & Brower, 1991), both to select the most stable products for in-house use and to be able to offer advice to others about which products will best meet their needs.

Polaroid Permanent-Color prints are the first color prints that can be considered to be truly "permanent," both when exposed to light during prolonged display and when stored in the dark. Permanent-Color prints, which can be made from color negatives, transparencies, or existing color prints, have images formed with special, highly stable color pigments instead of the dyes used in other types of color photographs. Making the prints is a fairly complex procedure that is best handled by specialized processing labs.

The classification of "ultra-stable" was proposed to describe the outstanding stability characteristics of the then-new Polaroid ArchivalColor process (later renamed the Polaroid Permanent-Color process) and to differentiate this extraordinary level of stability from the less stable ANSI "archival" classification that is applied to acetate- or polyester-base silver gelatin films. Materials included in the proposed "ultra-stable" group were black-and-white photographs on polyester-base film or fiber-base paper with toned silver gelatin images (light and dark storage); Polaroid Permanent-Color prints (light and dark storage); Ilford Cibachrome, Kodak Dye Transfer, and Fuji Dyecolor (dark storage only). Black-and-white RC prints, acetate-base films, and polyester-base films or fiber-base papers with untoned silver images were excluded from the ultra-stable classification (Wilhelm, 1987).

Although subject to light fading, Ilford Cibachrome polyester-base prints and color microfilm also can be considered permanent when kept in the dark; this property makes Cibachrome unique among conventional (simple to process) color materials. Under commonly encountered dark-storage conditions, Cibachrome polyester-base materials should last far longer than most black-and-white photographs.

Editor's note: Revised January 1991.

REFERENCES

Calhoun, J. M. (1952). Cold storage of photographic film. *PSA Journal, Section B: Photographic Science and Technique, 18B*(3), 86-89.

Calhoun, J. M. (1952). Storage of nitrate amateur still-camera film negatives. *Journal of the Biological Photographic Association, 21*(3), 1-13.

Severson, D. G. (1986). The effects of exhibition on photographs. In M. S. Holden (Compiler), *Topics in photographic preservation, vol. 1* (pp. 38-42). Washington, DC: American Institute for Conservation Photographic Materials Group, American Institute for Conservation. A slightly revised version was reprinted in *Picturescope, 32*(4), 133-135.

Wilhelm, H. (1981). Monitoring the fading and staining of color photographic prints. *Journal of the American Institute of Conservation, 21*(1), 49-64.

Wilhelm, H., & Brower, C. (1991). *The permanence and care of color photographs: Prints, negatives, slides, and motion pictures.* Grinnell, IA: Preservation Publishing.

Wilhelm, H. (1987 February). *Polaroid archival color: A progress report on a new, ultra-stable color print process.* Unpublished paper presented at the AIC Photographic Materials Group meeting, New Orleans, LA.

SARA WOLF GREEN

Conservator
The Textile Museum
Washington, D.C.

Managing Textile Collections

INTRODUCTION

A discussion of the care of textiles in a proceedings concerned primarily with library and archive collections may seem somewhat out of place. However, experience and observation show us that few collecting institutions have been able, historically, to stick to their specific acquisitions mission, even if that mission is stated rather than merely implied.

As the responsibilities of collections care have become more complex, it has been necessary to evolve management concepts that organize and prioritize activities related to collection preservation, security, and accessibility. The truly disastrous situations stemming from nonexistent collections management policies or improper use or maintenance of collection materials tend to be the cases which make national news. However, the simple neglect of collections held in the public trust, regardless of their real or perceived value, constitutes a direct attack to the foundation of those ideas and ideals which are embodied in terms like *cultural patrimony*.

Surely, the deterioration of a diary kept by a pioneer woman on the lonely, wind-swept plains of the early nineteenth-century American West does not threaten civilization. Certainly, greater menaces are an increasing lack of clean air and water, a deteriorating ozone layer, worldwide hunger, and economic and political instabilities. And yet, art, literature, and music are our humanity: the translation of the living to representation.

In his 1987 address, "The Moral Imperative of Conservation," Librarian of Congress James H. Billington spoke eloquently of the absolute necessity to preserve the artifacts of civilization because they embody that civilization's collective memory: "The authentically preserved artifact or text presents us with instructions about where we are

113

and where we might be going as well as where we have been" (Billington, 1987, p. 3). But it is the artifact, not the idea, that must be preserved. It is the artifact that makes possible the instruction.

How do textiles fit into such an existential interpretation of cultural patrimony? If existence and humanity can be defined in terms of Homer or Hemingway, textiles are at least a partial definition of humanness. To use clothing as a very simple example, textiles both create individuality and definition, as in a one-of-a-kind, designer evening gown; or supply anonymity and inclusion, as in a military uniform.

If the case has been made for the necessity of preserving textiles, a mechanism must be provided to support that goal. In order to develop a preservation strategy, the fundamental causes of the deterioration of those materials must be understood, as well as the techniques which are available for eliminating, or at the very least, slowing down the deterioration processes.

THE NATURE AND PROPERTIES OF TEXTILE FIBERS

The term *textile* requires a very broad definition. Even in those items made only from natural products, textiles can be found in forms as diverse as 200 yards of finely beaten bark to clothe a Fijian chief, or the meticulously embroidered and jeweled silks and velvets of Henry VIII. They are as humble and ordinary as the most simple quilt or as spectacular as a finely worked piece of lace.

The survival of any ancient textile is rather miraculous. Those which by luck of the draw have escaped destruction by ordinary use, and saved because of historical or sentimental attachment, have been subjected to other deteriorative forces including light, fluctuations of temperature and relative humidity, airborne pollutants, insect pests, the manufacturing process, or the inherent fragility of the materials themselves.

General Properties of Fibers

Fibers are the basic materials of which textile yarns and fabrics are created. While more and more examples of synthetic or man-made fibers can be found in collections which have special requirements for their preservation, natural fibers of plant and animal origin still compose the bulk of textile materials.

Textile fibers must have certain characteristics which make them suitable for manufacture into thread and eventually fabric. Fibers must have a sufficient length to allow them to be twisted about one another (spun), flexibility, strength to withstand the spinning and weaving process, and a certain amount of resilience.

Cellulose, the basic material of *cotton* and *linen* textiles, is a linear polymer composed of thousands of units of the simple sugar glucose. The fiber is easily damaged by acids but has excellent resistance to alkaline solutions. In general, cellulose has poor elasticity and resilience, which explains its tendency to wrinkle easily. Cellulose is a readily absorbent fiber and so is readily attacked by fungi such as mildew. Neither cotton nor flax (linen), however, are attractive to insects, although insects such as moth and carpet beetle will chew through cellulosic fibers to get to woolens or silks nearby.

Both cotton and linen are damaged and yellowed by exposure to light, and gradually lose strength through light deterioration. Both fibers gain strength when wet, which makes their handling during cleaning processes easier than, for example, silk, which loses strength in water. Because of its cylindrical fiber shape, cotton has greater elasticity than flax, the fibers of which are flatter in cross-section. As they age, flax fibers that have been folded, either for storage or as part of the fabric construction or use, tend to break along crease lines.

Protein fibers are obtained from animal sources and fall into two groups: hair fibers (from sheep, goat, camel, llama, alpaca and vicuna), and the secretions obtained from the larvae of the silk worm (bombyx mori). The hair fibers have some properties in common with the silk fibers, but some characteristics are quite different.

Protein fibers are composed of high molecular weight polypeptide chains of amino acids. These fibers tend to have excellent moisture absorbency but become weak when wet. They are fairly resistent to attack by acids but easily damaged by alkalis and oxidizing agents such as chlorine bleaches. As with cellulosics, sunlight causes the embrittlement and yellowing of protein fibers.

Because of its molecular arrangement and natural crimp, *wool* fibers and yarns have tremendous elasticity. When new, this allows for a great ability to stretch and then return to the relaxed state. As the fibers age, however, the ability to return to the relaxed state lessens, and distortions become permanent. Wool fibers are also readily subject to damage by agitation or abrasion in combination with heat and moisture. This property allows for the making of felt but can as easily cause irreversible damage during the process of wet cleaning.

Silk is composed of the protein fibroin, which is characterized by a high degree of molecular orientation that accounts for its tremendous fiber strength. It has tremendous absorption properties which account for ease of dyeing, but also makes it easily stainable. The ability of silk to absorb materials is also responsible for its deterioration. During the nineteenth-century in particular, a variety of bulking agents made primarily from metallic salts, were added to silk to give it both weight and a crisp hand. Because it was sold by the weight of the fabric, the bulking or "weighting" agents were added in the greatest amounts possible. Unfortunately, these materials, which are now chemically bonded to the fabrics, are the elements of their destruction. Weighted silk is commonly found in museum collections as costume and in many quilts. It is easily recognizable as it splits and powders of its own accord, quickly weakening and deteriorating under exhibition lights and breaking with even the most careful handling. All silks, and especially weighted silk, also are readily degraded by heat.

Because they are composed of proteins, hair fibers and silk are attractive food to insect pests. The most destructive are the clothes moth and carpet beetle. Both lay eggs within protein fabrics, and the larvae then eat their way to adulthood by consuming the fabric. If left unchecked, the insects will happily produce generation after generation until the textile is totally consumed.

THE EFFECTS OF THE ENVIRONMENT ON TEXTILE MATERIALS

Light

All materials of plant or animal origin (organic materials) can be damaged by light. Anyone who has stayed on the beach too long does not need to be convinced of the effects of overexposure to light. More and more, it is being convincingly demonstrated that the harm suffered from the exposure and burning of skin is an accumulated effect that eventually results in permanent, irreversible damage, like wrinkling or loss of skin tone. Light deterioration to most museum textiles may not be as quickly visible as a sunburn, but, like the effects on human skin, the accumulated damage will eventually appear as a change of color. The effects of light, however, are not confined to the fading of colors. The strength of textiles may also be affected by light, which acts to weaken and embrittle fibers.

The portion of the light spectrum that is of concern to the caretakers of textile collections includes ultraviolet, visible, and to a lesser degree, infrared radiation. These wavelengths of light can be found in greater or lesser amounts in natural daylight, and fluorescent and incandescent light bulbs. Only the visible portion of the light spectrum is critical to the perception of color in textiles. Clearly, then, there is much to be gained and nothing to be lost by eliminating the ultraviolet and infrared portions of the light spectrum.

Infrared radiation, or radiant heat, is controlled by the placement of lighting equipment at a sufficient distance from exhibited textiles so that the heat will be naturally dissipated into the surrounding air space. Likewise, lighting in display cases must be vented to prevent heat buildup.

Ultraviolet radiation, the most damaging part of the light spectrum, can be completely eliminated by the use of filters which are available for windows and fluorescent light tubes. UF-3 plexiglass, manufactured by Rohm and Haas, is an example of a filtering material which eliminates the ultraviolet portion of the light spectrum. The filters, available as clear acrylic sheets, can be used as replacement window panes, the construction material for exhibition casework, or as coverings for fluorescent tubes. Filtering plexiglass is available from most plastics suppliers. Low uv-emitting fluorescent lights, available from Verilux, Inc. in Greenwich, Connecticut can also be substituted for regular fluorescent tubes.

While it is possible to lessen the effects of light deterioration by the elimination of the ultraviolet portion of the spectrum, prolonged exposure as well as the intensity of visible light will, in time, produce the same effects of fading and embrittlement as a shorter time of exposure to ultraviolet radiation. It is necessary, then, to control both the intensity or brightness of light and the amount of time of exposure. The international museum community has strongly recommended that extremely light-sensitive materials, such as textiles and costumes, paper materials (prints, drawings, manuscripts), watercolors, dyed leathers and most natural history specimens, including botanical materials, fur, and feathers, be displayed at a maximum illuminance of 50 lux, or approximately 5 foot candles (Thomson, 1978, p. 23).

The length of time a textile is exposed to light is much more problematic and is somewhat dependent upon the individual characteristics of various materials. Silk, for example, is more quickly degraded by light than cotton, and some modern synthetic dyes are more light-stable than certain natural dyes. The rule of thumb employed at The Textile Museum for exhibition planning is the following: the display period for textiles should be no longer than six months and as limited as six weeks for more delicate materials.

Light Monitoring Equipment

Appropriate levels of illumination cannot be determined without the aid of light meters. In addition, filters must be periodically checked to ensure that the ultraviolet filtering capabilities have not been exceeded. While the acrylic filters are very long-lasting, they are eventually degraded by light and will have to be replaced. Both light-intensity meters and uv monitors are available in a range of styles and prices. Some research and investigation may be necessary to determine which monitors are appropriate for one's own institution. The Canadian Conservation Institute publication, *Recommended Environmental Monitors for Museums, Archives and Art Galleries* (Lafontaine, 1980) provides an excellent introduction to the topic, as well as a list of equipment suppliers in the United States and Canada.

Temperature and Relative Humidity

While temperature itself has less impact on textile preservation than relative humidity, excessively high temperatures contribute to fabric deterioration. Silk, for example, is readily degraded by heat, and the embrittlement of fibers is exacerbated by high temperatures. Biological activity also increases with heat. In terms of climate control, however, fluctuations of temperature impact levels of relative humidity. In general, as temperatures rise, relative humidity drops, and conversely, as temperatures drop, relative humidity rises.

While alive, plant and animal fibers are composed largely of water. While the amount of moisture is reduced when those fibers are no longer living, they retain the ability to absorb as well as lose moisture to the environment as humidity rises and falls. For textiles, the loss of moisture contributes to a loss of flexibility and, eventually, breakage. The absorption of moisture beyond the level of equilibrium that the manufactured textile has achieved results in dimensional change which often is visible as sagging and wrinkling.

Appropriate climate control is extremely difficult to achieve in the institutional setting. Volumes have been written about the subject, but the goal of maintaining specific levels of temperature and relative humidity with little or no fluctuation is nearly impossible or, at the very least, extremely expensive and generally impractical. In historic building in particular, the structures are not designed to withstand the effects of moderate levels of relative humidity (around 50 percent) during the winter season when natural levels of humidity reach levels of 15 or 20 percent with heating that is comfortable to both visitors and staff. Raising the humidity results in condensation on pipes and window glass, as well as within the fabric of the building structure, which may cause significant damage to the building itself.

While the issue of climate control poses many more problems than solutions, minimum goals are the maintenance of temperature and humidity with a minimum of daily or weekly fluctuations.

Airborne Pollutants

The two classes of airborne pollutants that are of concern in textile collections are particulate (dust and dirt, textile fibers and skin fragments from visitors, and minute fragments of metals which are the residues of the burning of fuels), and gaseous materials.

Dust contains minute abrasive particles, such as silicates (sand) and salts which are abrasive and can cut into fibers, particularly as yarns move against each other when handled, or when levels of relative humidity rise or fall. In addition, dust is a hygroscopic material which attracts acidic pollutants from the atmosphere and holds them on the textile surface.

Skin fragments and other textile fibers deposited on the surface of textiles as components of dust are not necessarily harmful in and of themselves, but are attractive to insects. Metals, such as iron, are readily corroded by atmospheric moisture, and could cause staining if concentrated in the dust on the surface of a textile.

A specific problem of new buildings containing concrete is the dusting of extremely fine particles which are extremely alkaline (Thomson, 1978, pp. 126-128) and can damage dye stuffs and silk. Because it can take as much as two years for alkalinity levels to drop sufficiently in a new building, concrete must be sealed to prevent damage to textile collections.

There is a good deal of information in conservation literature about the deteriorating effects of sulfur dioxide, ozone, nitrogen oxides, and chlorides. The oxidation of atmospheric sulfur dioxide creates sulfuric acid, which attacks cellulosic materials. In the presence of high humidity, deterioration is more rapid. Protein materials, especially silk, are weakened by exposure to sulfur dioxide. Ozone is a strong oxidant which destroys almost all organic materials and is especially harmful to cellulose and certain dyes. Nitrogen dioxide deteriorates indigo dyes and other dye stuffs containing amine groups. Chlorides are a particular problem for textiles which have been embellished with metallic threads, as the salts exacerbate metallic corrosion.

More recently, conservators have become aware of the damaging effects of formaldehyde emissions from building materials, paints, and varnishes which are often used in storage and exhibition furniture (Hatchfield & Carpenter, 1978). While the most dramatic form of deterioration caused by the formation of formic acids takes place on lead-containing alloys, such as bronze, formaldehyde is known to be responsible for causing cross-linking in proteins. Formic acid can also affect the pH of cellulose, as well as the color of certain pigments.

Eliminating formaldehyde-containing materials from the museum environment is extremely difficult, as they are contained in the adhesives of processed woods such as plywood and particle board, as well as coatings on paper-based laminates, and in certain paints and varnish coatings.

Insect Pests

As already stated, the clothes moth and carpet beetle are the most likely insects to cause damage in textile collections. As the long-term effects of insect repellent sprays are unknown, and since there is great concern about the health hazards of using poisons for the eradication of insect pests, more passive approaches to insect control are being investigated.

The best prevention of insect infestation is still proper maintenance. All textiles coming into an institution should be carefully inspected for evidence of damage, as well as eggs or other signs of infestation. As part of routine processing, textiles should be vacuumed front and back, and for costumes, even into seams and pockets to ensure that no live organisms or eggs are allowed to enter collection storage areas. While the brush attachment is useful for vacuuming carpets and other textiles with dense surfaces or pile, more fragile textiles should be vacuumed through plastic or fiberglass screen.

All institutions should have a pest-monitoring program in place as part of preservation strategy. For example, Integrated Pest Management (IPM) courses are available through the Workshop Series at the Smithsonian Institution's Office of Museum Programs. Nonpoisonous sticky traps should be placed along baseboards and checked monthly for evidence of insect activity.

If an infestation does occur, freezing has been found to be an extremely effective and safe method of insect eradication. Textiles should be placed in polyethylene "zip-top" type bags with as much air removed as possible and placed for forty-eight hours in a freezer which will reach a temperature of at least −2 to −4°F (Florian, 1986). To be absolutely certain of a 100 percent kill, the textile should be removed to a warm location for four days and then refrozen for an additional forty-eight hours. While there is little chance that the insect eggs will have survived the first freezing, the warming effect should be confusing enough to fool the growth process and allow the eggs to hatch. The second freezing then will complete the kill.

Exhibition

Because of the extremely deleterious effects of light on textiles, exhibition times should be kept to a minimum, light sources should be filtered for ultraviolet emissions, and all daylight should be excluded. The other factor to consider for textile display is the method of hanging and support.

Textile mounts are a subject which requires a great deal of discussion. Each textile has to be evaluated in terms of its condition and structure for a mount type to be selected.

Few mounts can be constructed without the use of a needle and thread. Stitching a textile to a support fabric, or even the rather simple process of applying a hanging strip of velcro require an interventive kind of treatment that is best carried out by a trained conservator. Most textile conservators find it extremely difficult to successfully make this point unless a fabric is seriously degraded, because minimal sewing skills are easy to achieve and textiles are, for the most part, so much a part of the common experience that mounting appears to be a simple and straightforward process. In many cases, the process is very straightforward, but as with any hand skill, a certain amount of training and experience is necessary if the textile is to be safely and adequately supported.

Storage

The storage of textile collections presents a complex series of problems that are common to all types of collection materials. The function of storage is the preservation of specimens in a stable, accessible state so that they will be available for use at some point in the future.

There are three aspects of storage that need to be identified for each object: packaging materials, containers, and cabinetry. **Packaging materials** for textiles include padding, interleaving, and wrapping materials. The most commonly used packaging materials are other fabrics (such as muslin) and archival tissues (both buffered and unbuffered). In some instances, materials like polyethylene, mylar, and nonwoven synthetic fabrics (such as pelon, reemay or polypropylene) are used as dustcovers. The most important specifications for packaging materials are that they be stable, preferably neutral, or if not completely neutral, at least chemically compatible with the textiles they package.

The choice of acid-free archival paper products for textile storage should be carefully made. The presence of alkaline buffered paper in the marketplace has been sufficient to allow an assessment of its importance in protecting cellulosic materials from wood and other wood-pulp paper products, but the effects of that paper's alkalinity on degraded protein materials has not been thoroughly measured. The warnings issued by photographic conservators regarding the deleterious effects of storing photographic prints in contact with alkaline-buffered materials should, however, suggest caution.

Textiles are not able to maintain their own shape and thus require some kind of support or container for storage. Even a flat textile, such as a sampler, requires some kind of container or support if it needs to be moved, since it is important to avoid any unnecessary flexing of aged or deteriorated fibers.

The best way to store flat textiles is in a flat state, supported by some auxiliary material, such as a mat or box, to facilitate movement. Textiles that are too large for one person to comfortably handle, or larger than cabinetry drawers or shelves, cannot be practically stored flat. Oversized textiles can often be stored in a rolled format. Carpets and tapestries, for example, may be rolled over an archival support tube, following the direction of the warp. Rolling should be neither tight (to prevent strain or stretching of the warp threads) nor loose (to prevent creasing or slipping of one layer against another), and the roll should be secured with soft ties made from a material such as white cotton twill tape.

Pile carpets should be rolled in the direction of the pile with the pile side in to prevent the knots from being spread apart and distorted. Any textile that has been lined should be rolled with the lining in, since it is virtually impossible to keep two or more layers perfectly registered. If creases must be formed, it is preferable for the creases to be located in the lining rather than the textile. Textiles with linings, embroideries, and other textiles with uneven or raised surfaces may need to be carefully padded, for example, with archival tissue, if they are to be rolled. Every attempt should be made to achieve an even, level surface in the roll to alleviate strain and creasing.

Rolled textiles should be covered with some kind of protective material before the ties are added to prevent the transfer of acidic hand oils and to protect the textile from dust, and possibly from light. Washed muslin fabric, archival tissue, nonwovens (such as reemay), mylar, and polyethylene have all been successfully used for covers. The choice of a covering material depends on the nature and properties of the textile materials themselves; their condition, the requirements for visibility and identification of the rolled textile, and the levels of environmental controls for both relative humidity and particulate. For example, mylar might be an appropriate choice if a slightly rigid covering over the textile is desired. However, that material can develop a static charge which would attract dust, especially if humidity levels are low and the heating and air conditioning system does not have sufficient particulate filters.

It is sometimes more appropriate to fold multilayered textiles.

Quilts are an example of a multilayered fabric that can be folded and then placed in an archival storage box or placed in a fabric wrapping for storage (Green, 1985). While folding a quilt helps to alleviate the crushing of heavily stuffed areas and strain on the quilting stitches that would occur if the piece were rolled, crease lines may develop if the folds are insufficiently padded. Crumpled archival tissue can be placed in the folds to increase the curve. Ideally, folded textiles should be inspected at least annually and the folds reoriented so that creases do not set in. Because of the need to handle this kind of textile routinely as part of its maintenance, only dimensional textiles in very sturdy condition should be handled in this way.

As with all storage decisions, the condition of the textile will dictate the proper storage method. For example, a carpet with a weakened foundation may be rolled pile out, or a quilt with tears may be more safely rolled than folded. Costumes present other sorts of problems, but like all other textiles, their condition will dictate the proper method of storage (Wolf, 1984). There has been a good deal of discussion over the years as to whether costumes should be laid flat or hung. The fact is that neither method is ideal, but both have specific and legitimate applications.

Knitted items, bias-cut clothing, and heavily beaded costumes are among the kinds of costume that should be stored flat in drawers, or in archival boxes designed to house costumes. (Costume boxes are generally sized at 30″ x 18″ x 6″ and are available from a variety of archival product suppliers, including but not limited to: University Products, P.O. Box 101, S. Canal Street, Holyoke, MA 01041; Process Materials Corporation, 301 Veterans Blvd., Rutherford, NJ 07070; Conservation Materials Ltd., Box 2884, 240 Freeport Blvd., Sparks, NV 89431.) The reason for this choice of storage format is that these items might stretch or tear under their own weight if hung. However, since these textiles are created as three-dimensional objects lacking internal supports, they must be padded to prevent creasing wherever a fold is introduced. And, as with all textiles stored flat, costumes should be placed on some kind of auxiliary material, such as a sheet of archival mat board, so that they will be supported when they are moved.

Hanging is often the preferred method of storing costume collections when space is at a premium. In addition, bulky or unusually constructed clothing, such as dresses with large bustles, can be most efficiently stored by hanging. The most important factor to consider with this storage method is that the entire weight of a garment will be supported by a relatively small area across the shoulder; consequently, only sturdy garments in good condition should be hung. Other considerations for a hanging cabinet or closet are placement of the bar high enough so that all garments clear the floor, and sufficient spacing between hangers so that the garments are neither compressed, creased, nor allowed to abrade each other when removed from the cabinet. Padded hangers should be used in hanging a garment. Padding should be resilient so that it does not compress under the weight of the garment, and bulky enough to increase the width of the hanging surface and reduce the stress on the shoulder seam without distorting the shape of the garment.

COLLECTIONS MANAGEMENT

The term *collections management* is about ten years old within the museum profession (Green & Denton, 1987). Like much of the conservation terminology, there is an implication that the definitions are universally understood. In fact, collections management has been defined and redefined in terms of each registrar's individual institutional situation, leaving little of the substance that originally defined the need for this specific approach to collections care. As a result, most of the writings on the subject tend to reduce the broad implications of management to isolated tasks like data entry or labeling specimens. While there is no need to redefine the term, it is useful to restate the goals of collections management in terms of their fundamental purposes: to provide a comprehensive and integrated approach whereby planning and implementation of management processes are applied to museum or other kinds of collections.

It is important to recognize that these functional areas do not exist in a vacuum, but are integral to all institutional activities. To reach the level of organization where collections management is functional within an institution, several policies and plans must be in place. The most important are a mission statement, a long-range plan, and a collections policy. Depending on the function and mission, an exhibitions policy may also be necessary.

The management aspects for collections are the mechanisms enabling specific functions to be accomplished. These functions are determined by the allocation and organization of institutional resources integral to the mission of the museum in interpretation and research. The five specific functional areas of collections management are planning, information systems, accessibility, physical environment, and monitoring & evaluation. While each of these areas is defined in terms of the tasks associated with its functions, on the management level they are highly interdependent, essential concerns of collections care. Looking at the various levels, the concerns of collections management might be listed as follows: *planning*—policies, manuals, and short & long-term goals and objectives; *Information Systems*—documentation, records, and research; *accessibility*—organization of collections, housing, and use; *physical environment*—security and safety, climate control, and pest management; and *monitoring & evaluation*—maintenance; and survey and inventory. (It is essential to eliminate the concept of collections maintenance from the primary definition of collections management function. Maintenance implies the preservation of the status quo rather than activities aimed at improving a situation. As such, maintenance is an area of monitoring and evaluation; it is a task rather than a function.)

The physical condition of collections has in large measure established the need for collections management. As such, the conservator has made an impact on the role of the collections manager in several ways. Because of work done by conservators and scientists to analyze the relationship between the products used in contact with objects and the various materials of collection specimens, ideal specifications have been developed for nearly every aspect of exhibitions and storage. The definitions of ideal climate control and pest management also evolving from conservation literature have become integral tasks of the management of the physical environment of collections.

While providing specification and definition to many of the roles of the collections manager, the principle tasks of the conservator are allied, rather than intertwined, with the tasks of the collections manager. The role of the conservator remains one principally of treatment, with an important component of providing the justifications as well as the specifications for certain aspects of collections care.

Depending upon the size of the institution and the training and capabilities of the staff, the tasks of collections management may reside with a variety of individuals. Regardless of who carries out these tasks, and regardless of the kind of collection, the overriding purpose of any collections management program is the preservation of the collection, embodied not only in the artifacts themselves, but in the products of planning (policies and manuals) and information systems (records, documentation and research), the consequences of physical environment (security and safety, climate control and pest management) and accessibility (organization of collections, use and housing), and the impact and benefits of monitoring and evaluation (maintenance, survey and inventory).

CONCLUSION

The materials a civilization collects—the books and manuscripts, paintings, musical scores and tapestries—are reflections of what that civilization is. These artifacts embody ideas and values, but they are much more than mere representations. Having read the following passage that a quilter's great-granddaughter quoted, one could hardly fail to understand the reasons for collecting and maintaining an otherwise anonymous textile:

> It took me more than twenty years, nearly twenty-five, I reckon, in the evenings after supper when the children were all put to bed. My whole life is in that quilt. It scares me sometimes when I look at it. All my joys and all my sorrows are stitched into those little pieces. When I was proud of the boys and when I was downright provoked and angry with them. When the girls annoyed me or when they gave me a warm feeling around my heart. And John, too. He was stitched into that quilt and all the thirty years we were married. Sometimes I loved him and sometimes I sat there hating him as I pieced the patches together. So they are all in that quilt, my hopes and fears, my joys and sorrows, my loves and hates. I tremble sometimes when I remember what that quilt knows about me. (Bank, 1979, p. 94)

REFERENCES

Bank, M. (1979). *Anonymous was a woman.* New York: St. Martin's Press.

Billington, J. (1987). The moral imperative of conservation. In J. S. Long (Ed.), *Invest in the American collection* (Proceedings from a regional forum on the conservation of cultural property at the Art Institute of Chicago, 16 June 1987) (pp. 1-16, in pocket). Washington, DC: The National Committee to Save America's Cultural Collections.

Florian, M. L. E. (1986). The freezing process—Effects on insects and artifact materials. *Leather Conservation News, 3*(1), 1-13.

Green, S. W. (1985). Maintenance and storage of quilt collections. *Conservation Notes #14.* Austin, TX: Texas Memorial Museum, University of Texas.

Green, S. W., & Denton, P. L. (1987, September). Unpublished presentation to the faculty of the Pilot Training Program in Collections Care for History Museums, Panhandle-Plains Museum, Canyon, TX.

Hatchfield, P, & Carpenter, J. (1978). *Formaldehyde: How great is the danger to museum collections?* Boston, MA: Center for Conservation and Technical Studies, Harvard University Art Museums.

Lafontaine, R. H. (1980). *Recommended environmental monitors for museums, archives and art galleries.* Technical Bulletin #3. Ottawa: Canadian Conservation Institute, National Museums of Canada.

Thomson, G. (1978). *The museum environment.* London: Butterworths.

Wolf, S. J. (1984). Storing costume collections. *Conservation Notes #8.* Austin: Texas Memorial Museum, University of Texas.

MARY LYNN RITZENTHALER

Supervisory Conservator
National Archives and Records Administration
Washington, D.C.

The Challenge of Archival Preservation

INTRODUCTION

The field of archival preservation is increasingly recognized as an area of specialization within the broader discipline of preservation of artistic and cultural works. Archival preservation is akin to both fine art and library preservation; but, while it shares common approaches and philosophical concerns with each of these fields, there are also several important differences. In large part, these differences relate to the nature of archival materials. Unlike fine art collections, archival records are generally intended to be used and handled by a variety of researchers. Although there are possibilities for duplicating or reformatting unstable or fragile records, large quantities of archival materials in original formats still must be capable of being used and handled. Paper must flex and bindings must function as vehicles both to protect and to allow access to information. Fine art holdings—even study collections—are subjected to much less (and less rigorous) handling than are archival materials.

Unlike library materials, archival records are most often unique; they do not exist in other formats, editions, or repositories. Issues of mass and scale also enter into the equation. While library collections often consist of hundreds of thousands of individual titles, archival holdings generally consist of such large numbers of individual items that archival series are measured in linear feet, not by the number of discrete pieces. Further, the value or significance of archival records tends to reside with groups and their relationship to one another, rather than in individual documents, although there are obviously exceptions to this generalization. The library preservation problem has been popularized almost exclusively as the brittle book problem. While archival repositories contain a good measure of brittle paper, archival records are just as likely to have been recorded on good quality papers that have retained their strength and flexibility over time.

ARCHIVAL PRESERVATION PROGRAMS

The characteristics of archival records briefly described—that is, uniqueness, size of holdings, and the relation of individual parts to the whole—have influenced the development of archival preservation programs. The complexity and diversity of archival records have also had great impact on the preservation challenge. Archival records are composite objects that reflect the history of technology and the ingenious ways that have been devised to record information over time. Materials composing archival records range from animal skins, such as parchment, to a wide variety of paper types manufactured for different purposes. Ledger papers, tissue papers found in letterpress copy books, tracing and drawing papers used for architectural renderings, bond and writing papers, and coated paper used for graphic works are but a sampling of the types of papers found in archival holdings. In addition to skin and paper materials used as supports for recorded information, metals, glass, and plastic films are also common substrates for archival records. Media used to record information are equally diverse and include graphite and colored pencils; carbon, iron gall, and numerous modern solvent- and water-based manuscript inks; printing and typewriter inks; pigments; and also photographic imaging methods. Magnetic media used to create computer tapes and video and sound recordings expand and complicate the problems of archival preservation. The abundance and variety represented by archival records have necessitated the development of multifocus preservation programs designed to meet the needs of diverse and disparate materials.

Archival preservation activities may be clustered into several programmatic areas: provision of a stable storage environment; copying, duplicating, and reformatting; controlling access and use; disaster preparedness; and conservation treatment. Remarks here will be limited to two of these areas, which are closely related: holdings maintenance and conservation treatment.

Holdings Maintenance

Holdings maintenance is a term that was devised at the National Archives to describe a range of basic preservation activities that are designed to prolong the useful life of archival records and defer expensive laboratory treatment by ensuring a stable storage environment. In the macro storage environment, temperature and relative humidity are controlled at approximately 70°F and 45 percent relative humidity (RH). (The temperature and relative humidity recommended is for mixed collections that are largely comprised of textual materials; other media, such as photographs and electronic records, have specialized storage requirements.) Holdings maintenance, which is actually concerned with the microenvironment in which records are stored, ensures that all storage enclosures coming into contact with record materials are stable and nonreactive over time. Holdings maintenance activities include rehousing archival records in file folders and boxes that meet National Archives specifications. Such paper and paperboard enclosures must be made from 100 percent fully bleached kraft pulp, be free of groundwood, have an alkaline reserve of 2 to 3 percent magnesium or calcium carbonate, and a pH between 8.0 and 10.0. In addition, enclosures intended to store photographic materials must pass the Photographic Activity Test as described in ANSI IT 9.2-1988. Other holdings maintenance actions include removing damaging fasteners, such as metals that rust or corrode, and the proverbial government red tape which contains dyes that are susceptible to bleeding. Fragile or damaged documents are placed in polyester L-sleeves with seals along two perpendicular edges to allow for safe placement and removal of weak paper. Holdings maintenance guidelines define the manner in which file folders and boxes should be filled in order to properly support and protect records. Provisions exist for removing oversize records to storage that will safely accommodate large dimensions and formats. Bound volumes with loose or detached spines or covers are tied with white cotton twill tape to keep component parts together. Photographic materials that are retained within textual files are lightly dusted and placed in polyester sleeves, both to protect them from handling and to segregate them from adjacent records. Given the difficulty of locating a consistent commercial source of ink that meets archival requirements (that is, ink that is nonacidic, nonbleeding, and colorfast), only graphite pencils are used to write notations on file folders. Pencils are a safer alternative at any rate, since it is not uncommon to find random, accidental marks made directly on the surface of record materials.

Preservation actions carried out under the mantle of holdings maintenance are intended to be performed by custodial archives technicians and archivists, rather than by conservation laboratory staff. It is important that all preservation actions be implemented consistently throughout an institution. For this reason, it is advisable to prepare written guidelines and to provide preservation training for all staff members.

There are a number of concrete benefits resulting from implementing a holdings maintenance program. Much damage to records occurs because of poor or inappropriate storage systems; improved housing practices will protect archival records and alleviate possibilities for damage. Replacement of unstable enclosures with paper and plastic materials of known good quality will eliminate sources of contamination that could otherwise increase the rate of degradation of archival records. Records in actual need of conservation treatment can also be identified during the course of performing holdings maintenance, making it possible to establish priorities and schedule necessary laboratory treatment.

Conservation Treatment

The primary goals of archival conservation treatment are to chemically stabilize and physically support archival records. Cosmetic improvement is generally not the overriding concern, although it is often a byproduct of treatment and may in fact be desirable for items required for exhibition or publication purposes. The quantity of most archival holdings makes it necessary to establish treatment priorities based on such factors as the condition, value, and intended use of the materials. Issues pertaining to value can be quite complex, since records requiring treatment may range from highly significant individual items—such as George Washington's inaugural address or the Emancipation Proclamation—to records of relatively low individual value, such as pension applications, military enrollments, or constituent mail. The assigned value of a record and its condition may be at great variance, at least in terms of treatment needs. An item of low intrinsic value may require a complex, time-consuming treatment, while a document of high intrinsic value may need nothing more than encapsulation. Given large quantities of records of varying value and condition and the fact that resources for conservation treatment are generally limited, it is necessary to set priorities, establish institutional policies, and develop good working relationships between archivists and conservators. Conservators can generally offer treatment options which range from stabilization and minimal intervention through complete treatment, without compromising the item. The latter point is very important, since most conservators working in the United States abide by the code of ethics and standards of practice adopted by the American Institute for Conservation of Historic and Artistic Works (AIC). Adherence to this code requires that all items be treated in accordance with a common high standard. Thus, while it would be inappropriate to take treatment shortcuts on an item of relatively low value, it would be permissible to perform a high quality but more limited range of treatment steps on the item to achieve the desired stabilization.

Single Item and Batch Treatments

The concepts of single item and batch treatments are still evolving in archival conservation. This dual approach was developed in response to the particular nature of archival records and the size of institutional holdings. Because of limited resources that must be used conscientiously to meet the treatment needs of large numbers of diverse materials, it is appropriate to allocate these resources in accordance with the varying values, intended uses, and condition of the items in question. However, it is important to understand that the attitudes and philosophy governing single item and batch treatments are the same. It is not intended that either the quality of treatment or materials used will be compromised, but rather that the degree or complexity of treatment be adapted to the specific needs of the records.

Single item treatments are normally reserved for individual records of great historical significance. Such records are likely to be institutional treasures and the focus of much institutional, scholarly, and constituent attention. Their value is such that it is mandatory to focus undivided attention on the item during the course of examination, testing, and all treatment steps. Examples of such highly important archival records will vary from institution to institution, but may include such items as constitutions or charters, treaties, and proclamations or speeches in the hand of historically important individuals. Another reason for selecting single item treatment involves the complexity of the treatment required in relation to the physical and chemical stability of the item. The nature of the component elements of a document, such as media, the presence of adhesives, and the type and condition of the support will also affect the choice of treatment approach and whether it is likely to be more or less intrusive or relatively passive. Single item treatments may be very complex, and may also be undertaken in experimental situations where treatment innovations are being explored that must be closely monitored.

On the other hand, *batch treatments* are reserved for groups of records—generally of moderate to low value—that exhibit the same qualities and require the same treatment steps. Therefore, one must know that all of the individual items in a batch have relatively the same value and that the materials composing them are the same. For example, a group of letters written in iron gall ink on early nineteenth-century machine-made papers could be handled as a treatment unit, as could a series of court transcripts or application forms consisting of printer's and manuscript inks on groundwood paper. Batch treatments should be reserved for groups of like materials that require relatively routine treatments. The number of items in a batch may vary, but could easily consist of groups of five, twenty-five, or even two hundred items. Parenthetically, it should be noted that batch treatment is not mass treatment, which implies treatment on a much larger scale. Further, in batch treatment a group of documents would possibly be subjected to a number of treatment steps, whereas *mass treatment,* as the term is commonly used, refers to a large number of items being exposed to a single treatment operation.

Other basic differences that exist between single item and batch treatments relate to time expended on a single archival record and the degree and type of documentation employed. All archival institutions must expend available treatment hours judiciously. While it is overly simplistic to state that single item treatments take more time than do batch treatments, it is true that complex treatments, or those that are not employed on a regular basis, generally take more time to execute than do more routine treatments. A routine treatment, such as removal of dirt by surface or dry cleaning, can suddenly become complex if the paper is weak or the medium is friable. Usually, however, single item treatments are more time-intensive. For example, it may be possible to perform humidification, flattening, and rehousing on a batch of 500 trifolded records in a period of forty hours. That same forty hours could be expended on treating a single architectural drawing that required dry cleaning, washing, and lining. Given the diversity of archival materials, there is clearly a need for both approaches in an archival conservation program.

Documentation

Conservators are required to document the treatments they carry out. This is another area in which there are differences between archival and library and fine art conservation. The AIC code of ethics requires that all treatments be fully documented. That is, there should be a written condition description, treatment proposal, and treatment report for every item treated, in addition to photographic documentation before and after treatment. Such recordkeeping is necessary for significant archival records as well as for significant treatments, and it is therefore standard practice for single item treatments. Such an approach is not feasible, however, for batch treatments, given the nature of the materials and the routine types of treatments performed. It would be entirely possible in such situations for recordkeeping to take more time than the actual treatment. Therefore, most batch treatments are documented by use of some type of form or checklist (either manually created or computer-assisted) to describe the treatment steps performed and all materials used. The concept of levels of documentation is one which archival and library conservators are currently discussing within the context of AIC.

CONCLUSION

Decision-making regarding the appropriate implementation of single item versus batch treatment requires close communication between archivists and conservators. The values assigned to records, the relationships among groups of records, and the uses to which the records will be put over time must all be considered in order to make sound conservation treatment decisions. Despite the previously described differences between single item and batch treatments, there is another important characteristic they share. Decisions regarding the type and level of treatment to be carried out must be based upon the evaluation of individual records. While it is possible to make generic observations and decisions regarding a series of records and then to group them into appropriate batches, it is still necessary to actually look at individual records to assure their suitability for the treatment envisioned. This issue relates back to some basic characteristics of archival records, namely, their diversity and uniqueness. Despite efforts to standardize and categorize archival records, they do not always cooperate! It is not unlikely, therefore, to encounter several pieces of parchment in a box containing what was presumed to be all eighteenth-century paper. Obviously, the results could be disastrous if the parchment were overlooked in a treatment that specified washing the entire contents of the box. In a similar vein, a document of extremely high intrinsic value could be interfiled with a group of documents of much less significance. If its existence were not noted during the review of records prior to treatment, the results could be equally inappropriate.

Any time that a particular treatment approach becomes something of a standard procedure, there is a danger that the treatment system will begin to take on a life of its own. In such cases, treatments can be applied inappropriately or unnecessarily if the records are not reviewed carefully prior to treatment and individual decisions are not made. This phenomenon occurred to some degree when cellulose acetate lamination was the primary treatment of choice in some institutions. There is certainly the potential for such a situation when carrying out batch conservation treatments. Careful examination, evaluation, and testing will always form the basis for sound archival conservation, whether the work is carried out on a batch or on a single item basis.

MARY LYNETTE LARSGAARD

Assistant Head, Map and Imagery Laboratory Library
University of California at Santa Barbara

Conservation of Cartographic Materials

INTRODUCTION

Conservation and preservation of cartographic materials are a challenge chiefly because so many different media are to be found in what is modestly termed a map room — maps (flat, rolled, or folded), profiles, sections, diagrams, views, globes, atlases, remote sensing imagery (in many different forms, such as positives, negatives, roll film, and slides), plastic models, and just recently, data in digital form (magnetic tape, CD-ROM, and probably more to come). In fact, it often seems that the map room is home to any object that depicts a geographic area or carries cartographic information and is also awkward to handle. In the last ten years or so, conservation has had a greatly heightened image in the library world and, by extension, in the map library world. Consequently, map librarians have been forced to consider conservation far more than they did in the past, as evidenced by the appearance of columns on preservation and conservation in the leading map library journals, such as the *Information Bulletin* of the Western Association of Map Libraries, the *Newsletter* of the Association of Canadian Map Libraries, and *base line*, the newsletter of the American Library Association's Map and Geography Round Table (WAML, ACML, ALA MAGERT).

CARTOGRAPHIC MATERIALS ON PAPER

Most map librarians deal mainly with products on paper. Paper can be extremely stable, depending upon how it is made and how it is taken care of. As is commonly known, paper made of rags is remarkably long-lived; but paper made from ground wood, a highly acidic and deteriorative material, decays quite readily, as evidenced by newspapers, which may almost fall apart before one's eyes. While the maps received in the U.S. Depository Program, and especially those issued by the U.S. Geological Survey, are on reasonably good paper, still, those that came out during the early part of this century are becoming yellowed and brittle, as any map librarian can discover by a quick trip to the map cases.

An additional deteriorative element of twentieth-century library life is the extensive use of photocopying, some forms of which seem to be not just impermanent but close to evanescent. Blueline prints, especially, are burdens for the map librarian for two reasons: the ink fades when exposed to light, and the paper itself is often of poor quality and will readily discolor (usually yellowing) relatively quickly. It is thus singularly unfortunate that some state and foreign geological surveys, and some commercial firms (such as those dealing with oil well locations) use this form of reproduction frequently.

Generally speaking, black printing inks are permanent and will probably outlast the paper on which they are printed. But one must beware of other inks, such as nutgall, which will turn brown and fade out, weakening the paper on which they are printed. Fortunately, this type of ink appears in the main only in pre-1900 maps (Larsgaard, 1987, pp. 164-166).

The other major factor that affects the stability of paper is, as previously mentioned, the environment in which it is stored, including the methods of storage. Heat and light have deleterious effects on paper because paper deterioration is a chemical process, and any increase in energy input speeds up that process. The atmosphere in which paper is kept is therefore important, but not only for temperature; relative humidity is also of considerable interest, since paper is at its most durable at about 50 or 60 percent relative humidity, with lower humidities causing desiccation and high humidities inviting mildew and mold. Dust and sulfur dioxide in the air also do paper no good, nor do fungi, insects, rodents, or bacteria. Another hazard of environment is the physical location of the library; those sited on flood plains in tornado-prone areas obviously are at risk. Indeed, every library should have a disaster plan that takes into account what water and fire hazards exist and how to deal with them. Towards this end, Thomas Nagy (1984) wrote a disaster plan especially for the then National Map Collection of Canada.

Considering all of the above, the ideal map library would have items made out of rag paper, stored in pollutant-free air, in total darkness, with appropriate and constant temperature and humidity, housed in a fireproof structure on high ground, and with no organisms about, especially not human beings with their dirty, sweaty hands (Larsgaard, 1987, p. 170). However, the purpose of map libraries is to provide materials to be used, and the map librarian must figure out a way of making maximum use and maximum preservation come as close together as possible.

Everyday Handling, Care, and Storage

From the moment cartographic materials are received in the map room, their preservation is a primary concern. They should be un-wrapped carefully. As they are unpacked, the unpacker should note any delicate or high-use materials, which should be considered for encap-sulation or other treatment immediately, before they fall apart. After unwrapping, any rolled maps should be flattened; if the maps are not too tightly rolled, they may be reverse-rolled and left that way for a day or two, or just weighted down with cartography weights or any large, heavy books (bound *Congressional Records* work quite well). Maps that are at all brittle should not be reverse-rolled, since they will crack and tear; instead, they should go into a damp box with minimum dimensions of 49 inches x 36 inches x 8 inches, with a net about halfway up upon which items to be humidified are placed, along with a container with a sponge and some water in it. Failing that, the map librarian may use a large plastic garbage can with a pint of tepid water in a plastic container in the center. Unfortunately, this will work only for relatively small maps; the only recourse for larger maps is to take them home and leave them in a corner of the bathroom while one is taking a long, hot shower.

Particularly with the increase in thefts from libraries, or at least in the increasing number of reports of such thefts, a property stamp is essential; certainly a primary form of preservation is making sure that the items stay in the library. At a minimum, the stamp should contain the name of the institution and the date of receipt. A consistent location on items (e.g., lower righthand corner if the space is empty, the verso if it is not, and so on) must be selected. Certainly for rare materials, the map librarian will want to look into obtaining from the Assistant Director for Preservation at the Library of Congress a supply of black ink that is considered appropriate for use on such materials.

It is at this point, when classification and cataloging are performed, that the map librarian should have in mind a list of selective criteria based on the map room's collection development policy: which items are to be kept indefinitely, which items are "kamikaze" maps (purchased in multiple copies, with the tattered old ones being thrown out) and which will be kept by the library only for a restricted time period. For example, a map room in Kansas may well not wish to keep superseded U.S. Geological Survey topographic quadrangles of Vermont. This sort of decision making is best done in concert with other map librarians throughout the United States, so that it may be truly said that every cartographic object is kept in at least one place in the United States.

The cartographic object is at this point ready to be labeled (most often in pencil if directly on the object, or with a typed label if it is the container that is being labeled), and then sent to the filing cabinets. Cartographic materials should be kept in acid-free containers whenever possible; for maps, this generally means the use of acid-free paper folders, with up to about fifty maps per folder. Aerial photographs can be kept in acid-free envelopes and placed in metal filing cabinets or in acid-free boxes. When at all possible, maps should be kept unfolded, since every fold is a tear waiting to happen; photographs should never be folded, since this cracks the emulsion. While the vast majority of cartographic materials, maps and imagery, may be relatively easily dealt with using standard filing methods, the very large maps are a continuing trial to map libraries. Decisions on how to handle them ranging from sectioning them (as the Library of Congress does), to storing them rolled and then placing them horizontally, to encapsulating them under ultra-violet filtering acrylic sheeting and then suspending them from a wooden rod (Marley, 1988, p. 28).

A map librarian has several different types of storage to look at because of all the formats to be dealt with. For items such as maps, sections, diagrams, plans, and views, the decision overwhelmingly is to keep these items in metal files, usually horizontal but sometimes vertical in nature. The discussions as to which to use when seem to boil down to the vertical files being most appropriate when the items to be stored in them are all of approximately the same size (Larsgaard, 1987, pp. 172-176). It is after this point that life becomes more difficult.

Atlases are very nearly the easiest of the non-flatmap items to deal with; standard book shelving, with shelves relatively close together (about six inches apart) will work if the library cannot afford the relatively expensive roller shelving such as the Library of Congress has. As previously noted, aerial photographs are best preserved when they are each put in acid-free envelopes and then stored in acid-free boxes or in standard library vertical-file cabinets. Globes and plastic raised-relief maps are superb display items, and this is the best way to store them. Cartographic data in digital form are still somewhat of a mystery to most map librarians; at present, the best answer seems to be to store them in climate-controlled, low-temperature areas, and to keep in mind that the magnetic tapes are subject to data drift and must be rewound regularly (Larsgaard, 1987, p. 180). Microform is, mercifully, relatively easy to deal with; the map librarian may select standard microform cabinets.

Use

At this point, it behooves the map librarian to remember the object of all this work: that the items be used. The question then becomes how to keep use from becoming misuse. The most flagrant form of misuse is stealing, and the sad fact is that the only way to safeguard most cartographic materials is to have closed stacks. Anyone who doubts this need only read Harold Otness' (1988) blood-chilling " 'Going Plating:' Stealing Maps from Libraries." His main messages are well worth heeding: identify valuable maps, especially those in book-format publications; transfer them to a secure area; improve bibliographic control, especially on the shelflist, so that items may be identified as library property in the sad event of their loss; mark all items with the library property stamp; have users identify themselves when they are handling library property (e.g., have them produce a photo identification card) and check that ID carefully; conduct regular inventories; report all thefts promptly; keep a detailed chronological record of events if a theft occurs; and encourage stronger sentences for those who steal library materials.

Thinking more positively—that the item requested has not and will not be stolen—the next decision is whether the map room will allow checkout or photocopying. The map librarian should be fore-warned that checking a map out is very definitely an accelerated-aging process, so the value, stability, and frailty of the map must be considered. Any items to be loaned must be protected by being checked out in sturdy containers with stern instructions to the user that replacements will be required should the item be damaged. A form should be inserted with the item checked out that details for the user exactly how the item is to be reinserted in its container, and what sorts of damage will require replacement of the object. Another problem is that using a map for field work is not just accelerating its aging but rather guaranteeing its destruction. Should the borrower be recalcitrant about returning the item, it is frequently useful to point out the cost of a color reproduction or a replacement for the item.

Today, most users consider it a birthright to obtain photocopies, and in the main it is wise to humor them in this thought. The problem is that photocopying most cartographic materials is a bit difficult on a standard photocopier because it involves folding the item. Larger map collections are able to provide photocopiers that have removable tops so this folding does not occur. Individuals in charge of smaller collections can certainly strongly encourage that such photocopiers be obtained for the library as a whole, since it is not just cartographic materials that need oversize copies.

Libraries with rare, valuable maps can consider having negatives made of these items, and perhaps photocopies also, so that users browse the copies instead of the actual items, and so that copies can be made quickly and inexpensively upon request. Another option is to obtain facsimiles, using a directory of facsimile publishers (Noe, 1980).

One special sort of use of cartographic materials is putting them on display. If the item is a map or other flat cartographic material and framing is to be done, the framing should be museum quality, using acid-free board and tape; the item must not touch the glass. Light is injurious, as was formerly noted; items should not be left on display for long periods of time, and an ultraviolet shield should be used (Larsgaard, 1987, pp. 186-187).

Damage and Repair

Damage may be mechanical, chemical, or both. Perhaps the most common form of damage that map librarians see is tears. The next most common is some sort of yellowing and brittleness of paper. Librarians taking care of imagery may find spots, scratches, tape residue, and fading, especially on their older aerial photographs. Those librarians in map rooms that have microforms have already heard about using other than silver halide film, and are careful to read the literature and to watch for other problems. When it comes to damage to cartographic data in digital form, the field is so new that map librarians are reduced to falling back on the precepts used for other forms of cartographic material: handle it carefully, store it correctly, and search for literature explaining what such handling and storage is (e.g., DeWhitt, 1987), thus avoiding having to deal with any damage.

The rules for repair of cartographic materials are the same as for repairing other library materials: do only what is reversible; make sure that no information is lost during the repair procedure; and, unless the map librarian is also a trained conservator, keep the repairs simple ones. What most map librarians do, very sensibly, is to confine repairs to tears and to the removal of surface dirt. Tears may be repaired either by using archival-quality tapes or by using flour paste and tissue. The method used very much depends upon the value of the item being repaired; tape is never used on rare and valuable materials, but rather on such items as a U.S. Geological Survey topographic quadrangle that is in print and therefore relatively easily and inexpensively replaced.

Surface cleaning is another repair that map librarians may attack on their own. Dusting and washing of plastic models is easily done; the point at which one must be careful is when the plastic begins to get brittle with age, at which time the librarian should consider purchasing another copy if it is still in print, or filling the verso of the model with plaster of some kind. Cleaning dirt from maps involves working gently with an eraser or drafting a drycleaning pad and a brush; the item should be weighted down and work should proceed from the center, away from the weight. Dusting off a globe or occasionally cleaning it with a damp cloth is well within the abilities of most map librarians, but anything more detailed should probably be left to experts (Baynes-Cope, 1985). Imagery tends to be more difficult to work with than paper, since one is also dealing with an emulsion and often a nonpaper base; gently wiping off dust and grease pencil marks may mark the limits for most caretakers of these materials.

Another form of repair which is also an important form of microstorage is encapsulation in polyester film. Mounting, varnishing, and lamination are all out of favor in conservation circles, so any strengthening to be done for flat cartographic materials must be in almost all circumstances via encapsulation. Although the encapsulated object is heavier and thicker than the original (thus taking up more space in the file cases) and has a gloss, it has the tremendously important benefits of being relatively quick, easy, and inexpensive to do, and also of being strong and instantly reversible. In addition, it does not harm or change the original item in any way. The materials needed are polyester film (generally 3 mil, although 5 and 7 mil may be used to provide the necessary support for larger maps) and double-sided adhesive tape. Tools needed are a sharp knife or pair of scissors (the knife is better, since it enables one to make long, straight cuts), a few weights, a large table, a rubber roller (helpful but not essential), and a long metal straightedge. For each item to be encapsulated, two pieces of film about two inches longer and two inches wider than the item are cut; the item is centered on one piece of film, tape carefully placed at the outside edges of the film, the top protective cover of the tape peeled off, and the second piece of film placed on top, thus making a sandwich (*Polyester Film Encapsulation*, 1980; Rieke et al., 1984, p. 7).

While most map librarians will not want to proceed beyond these simple techniques, it is still a good idea for them to know what else can be done. The next level of repair procedures is that of washing the item; of course, the major problem with printed objects such as maps is that the print may well not survive a bath. A conservator considering washing a map will always test, with a small drop of water in an inconspicuous area, to see if inks are waterfast; color inks are particularly liable to blurring. What makes maps even more difficult to wash than other paper is their sheer size and the fact that finding supports for wet maps (since paper is far weaker when wet than when dry) may be almost impossible. Once the difficulties of finding a container and supports are conquered, one can proceed with soaking the map in cold water for about an hour, then drying it slightly, placing it between blotters, putting weights on top of the blotter, and leaving it to itself for three or four weeks (Akers, 1980; Larsgaard, 1987, p. 189).

Removing stains, varnish, and foxing are also techniques that require considerable expertise, not to mention a willingness to work with toxic chemicals. For example, removing adhesive-tape stains may require the use of benzene or carbon tetrachloride, and foxing may be removed only by bleaching with chemicals such as chloramine. Working with items that have colored inks makes any such procedure even more complicated, as can be clearly seen by reading "A Search for Procedures for Restoration and Stabilization of Sixteenth and Seventeenth Century Netherlands Atlases Damaged by Green Paint" (Blank et al., 1984). The problem in this particular case involved one hundred or so atlases that had severe brownness on the reverse of where green paint had been applied. The green paint itself was badly browned and the paper was brittle. After a considerable expenditure of time and materials— which included rapid aging of prepared model scraps of paper—the workers finally came up with a procedure: fix the paints, bleach the paper, wash in running water, neutralize with a bicarbonate solution, remove the film that fixed the paints, and impregnate the paper to strengthen it; then, if additional strengthening is needed, laminate the pages with tissue.

Another form of sophisticated conservation is that of deacidification. Deacidification attempts to lower the acid content of paper and thus prolong its life by introducing an alkaline chemical into the paper to neutralize the acid. The process used may be aqueous, nonaqueous, or vapor; and the discussions as to which is best have occupied a certain amount of library periodical space over the last few years, as the work done by the Library of Congress and by Wei T'o often appears in the pages of the library press. The final word as to whether the Library of Congress's Diethyl Zinc (DEZ) process or Wei T'o solution is best has yet to be pronounced. Given the state of library collections in the United States, with all having their share of brittle maps, it is a topic that must be viewed with interest.

It follows that when one has conservation or repair problems that one has not the technical expertise to cope with on one's own, one begins to look elsewhere and to wonder where one may have the work done. As mentioned previously, over the last ten years, libraries have shown considerably more interest in conservation than in any earlier time, with the result that larger libraries, especially in the university world, have conservation librarians or preservation representatives; the map librarian's life is made much easier if one of these persons is *in situ*. If there is no resident conservator, the next step is to check in issues of *AB Bookman*, or to ask conservators for the names and addresses of reputable firms. One encouraging sign is the establishment of conservation centers, such as the Northeast Document Conservation Center in Andover, Massachusetts, and the Centro di Studi per la Conservazione per la Carta, in Rome, Italy.

CONCLUSION

Working with cartographic materials requires that the map librarian become familiar with conservation and preservation methods for a wide variety of materials—globes, atlases, imagery (black and white; color), plastic models, maps, sections, views, diagrams, and so on. This, by extension, means that the map librarian must keep current on the methods of preservation for every sort of medium upon which cartographic data might conceivably appear, realizing at the same time that a substantial majority of all cartographic materials are on paper and will probably continue to be so for some years. (An appendix to this paper lists sources of equipment and supplies that are useful in the preservation of cartographic materials.)

The map librarian must recognize that conservation of cartographic materials depends upon correct methods of handling, storage, and display, and upon correct atmospheric controls for the area in which the collection as a whole is kept. Insofar as possible, the map librarian should select cartographic materials with an eye to their durability if they are to be kept for an extended period of time. Newly received items should receive repair or strengthening as their future use demands. The map librarian should be aware that a well-constructed collection development policy, preferably put together while keeping in mind the policies of other map collections, is an important part of a conservation program, not only for the individual library, but for the map library world as a whole.

When a cartographic item needs repair, the map librarian needs to look at it carefully and determine if such repair is within the technical abilities of the persons available to do the work, and if the item is of sufficient value—either now or in the future—that the work is worth doing; that is, would it be sufficient to preserve the information by microforming the item, or does the actual item have to be preserved? When repair is essential, the following principles must be observed:

— The process should be reversible.
— The process should use materials that are permanent and durable.
— The originality of the document should not be disturbed.
— Information should not be obscured or destroyed.
— The repair should be tidy, evident, but not obtrusive.
— The process should be appropriate to the item, and as inexpensive as possible while still keeping in mind the above principles.

In addition, the map librarian must remember that the map room is not just a warehouse but rather a place where items are meant to be used. And this is perhaps the most difficult: making sure that users find exactly the items they need and get the information they need without contributing substantially to the aging of the items. There is no way around the fact that use ages materials; what the map librarian must do is figure out ways so that valuable materials are handled as seldom as possible, that surrogates are available, and that multiple copies of heavy-use items (e.g., road maps of the city in which the library is located, U.S. Geological Survey sheets for the local area) are obtained.

The end result of all of this juggling of concepts should be a map room that can provide, for as along as the library is in existence, the cartographic material that users need. That result is worth the effort.

APPENDIX: ADDRESSES

I. Equipment

Hamilton Industries
1316 Eighteenth Street
Two Rivers, WI 54241

Mayline Company
627 North Commerce
Sheboygan, WI 53081

Plan Hold
17621 Von Karman Avenue
Irvine, CA 92714

Ulrich Planfile
2120 Fourth Avenue
Lakewood, NY 14750

Reflector Hardware Corporation
1400 N. 25th Avenue
Melrose Park, IL 60160

Spacesaver Corporation
1450 Janesville Avenue
Ft. Atkinson, WI 53538

Stacor Corporation
285 Emmet Street
Newark, NJ 07114

II. Supplies

Conservation Resources International
1111 N. Royal Street
Alexandria, VA 22314

University Products
P.O. Box 101
Holyoke, MA 01041

Hollinger
3810 South Four Mile Drive
Arlington, VA 22206

Wei T'o Associates
P.O. Drawer 40
Matteson, IL 60443

Light Impressions, Inc.
439 Monroe Avenue
Rochester, NY 14607-3717

REFERENCES

Akers, R. C. (1980). The cleaning and restoration of maps. *The Map Collector, 10* (March),19-23.

Baynes-Cope, A. D. (1985). *The study and conservation of globes.* Wien, Austria: Internationale Coronelli-Gesellschaft.

Blank, M. G.; Dobrusina, S. A.; & Lebedeva, N. B. (1984). A search for procedures for restoration and stabilization of sixteenth and seventeenth century Netherlands atlases damaged by green paint. *Restaurator, 6*(3), 127-138.

Book Preservation Technologies. (1988). Washington, DC: U.S. Office of Technology Assessment.

Cruse, L. (1985). Storage of maps on paper, microforms, optical disks, digital disks and magnetic memories. In E. Mount (Ed.), *Role of maps in sci-tech libraries,* (pp. 45-57). New York: Haworth Press.

DeWhitt, B. L. (1987). Long-term preservation of data on computer magnetic media, parts I and II. *Conservation Administration News (CAN), 29*(April), 7, 19, 28; *CAN, 30* (July), 4, 24.

Eastman Kodak Company. (1985). *Conservation of photographs.* Rochester, NY: Eastman Kodak Company.

Kathpalia, Y. P. (1973). *Conservation and restoration of archive materials.* Paris: UNESCO.

Larsgaard, M. L. (1987). *Map librarianship: An introduction* (2nd ed.). Littleton, CO: Libraries Unlimited, Inc.

Marley, C. (1988). Save it! Conservation/preservation news. *Association of Canadian Map Libraries Newsletter, 68*(September), 27-28.

Nagy, T. (1984). Disaster contingency planning for map collections: An ounce of prevention . . . *Association of Canadian Map Libraries Bulletin, 53*(December), 1-30.

Noe, B. R. (1980). *Facsimiles of maps and atlases: A list of reproductions for sale by various publishers and distributors* (4th ed.). Washington, DC: Library of Congress.

Otness, H. (1988). 'Going plating:' Stealing maps from libraries. *Western Association of Map Libraries Information Bulletin, 19*(4), 206-210.

Polyester Film Encapsulation. (1980). Washington, DC: Preservation Office Research Services, Library of Congress.

Rieke, J. L.; Gyeszley, S; & Steele, L. (1984). Preservation of sheet maps, lamination or encapsulation: A durability study. *Special Libraries Association Geography and Map Division Bulletin, 138*(December), 2-10.

Smith, R. D. (1987). Mass deacidification: The Wei T'o understanding. *College and Research Libraries News, 48*(1), 2-10.

Sturges, P. (1987). Policies and criteria for the archiving of electronic publishing. *Journal of Librarianship, 19*(3), 152-172.

Thompson, E. T. (1980). *Collecting and preserving architectural records.* Nashville, TN: American Association for State and Local History. (Technical Leaflet 132).

CARLA J. MONTORI

Head, Preservation Division
University of Michigan Library
Ann Arbor, Michigan

Preservation Planning:
The Vital First Step

INTRODUCTION

Concern over the preservation of cultural materials is not a new phenomenon, but wide-ranging institutional action to ensure that such preservation occurs is new. For years, institutions have employed conservators and technicians to provide single item treatment for materials damaged or vulnerable to damage. More recently, the trend has been to establish preservation programs that take a more holistic approach to the dizzying multitude of factors that, taken together, comprise the institution's preservation challenge.

For the most part, the first preservation programs in the nation's libraries were started only in the early 1970s. Staff at institutions supporting these early programs are responsible for developing the concept of a library-wide preservation effort that was not aimed solely — or even primarily — at rare books and special collections.

It is often quite easy to rouse people to a state of heightened awareness of and concern about the preservation challenge in an institution. Many librarians and archivists concerned with the range of problems caused by embrittled paper have grabbed an administrator's attention by crumbling a sheet of brittle paper and allowing the pieces to drift to the floor. As a matter of fact, the first stage of preservation consciousness is often a feeling of panic. This is not entirely bad. Certainly, it has its place as a way to galvanize reaction from peers who did not recognize the problems, and to convince administrators that the problems have to be addressed in an organized and rational manner. Panic does have its applications when the object is to stir emotions and elicit a strong reaction.

147

Another characteristic of panic is that, once a person has succeeded in getting others excited about the need to preserve the material in the collection, those same people are likely to come back to the initiator with the directive to get in there and do something about the problem. The questions are, of course, where does one begin, and how are the time, effort, and money best spent? Clearly, careful study of the nature and extent of the problem facing a particular institution is of paramount importance. A thorough assessment of the collection would include, but not necessarily be limited to, examination of the following: the formats represented in the collection; the age of the collection, or, rather, the range of ages of items in that collection; the physical condition of the material itself; the environment in which it is stored, and, if applicable, the differing environments in which it is displayed and used; the type of shelving and housing (such as boxes, racks, etc.); the patterns of use, and of misuse, if that is a problem; any inhouse programs for maintenance, refurbishing, reformatting, or conservation; and any established relationships with outside vendors of those same services.

Condition Surveys

In recent years, there have been a number of condition surveys conducted at research institutions around the country. In the library world, many of these surveys have concentrated on the effort to determine what percentage of a collection is brittle (with *brittle* being defined as the inability of paper to withstand two double folds of a corner of a page). Books printed on brittle paper cannot be used without the danger of loss of text. Horrifying statistics have been corroborated time and again at institutions around the country: 25 percent to over 35 percent of the collections of the nation's major research libraries are brittle. Many of these same libraries uncover other similarities as well regarding the type and condition of the building, the history of use and misuse of materials, and a sad history of inappropriate treatment. Yet, many libraries continue to conduct individualized surveys. Why?

Even though one can read published results of surveys done at other institutions, even though one can see that each survey only reinforces the findings of every other survey, there are still very good reasons for conducting a collection assessment at one's own institution. The results of such a survey allow the particular institution to prioritize its own needs; give very specific ammunition for budgetary purposes; provide information useful in dealing with physical plant, engineering, and housekeeping departments; and establish a baseline against which to measure progress. This last reason is very important. Progress can and will be made, although it is sometimes difficult to see on a day-today or even month-to-month basis. Preservation may not be the field to go into if one is looking for instant gratification.

Perhaps the most important point in favor of an institution conducting its own survey is that survey results are often the best, and sometimes the only, way to capture the attention of the higher administration, the people who control the budget. The collections in a library, archive, or museum are valuable resources representing and bringing together a huge investment of money and intellectual effort. Moreover, these same collections are often a great source of pride to the parent institution or community. How many times has a library been called the "heart of a university?" How often is it said that a museum enhances or forms the center of a city's cultural life? Data that proves the deterioration—or demonstrates the vulnerability to deterioration of a particular institution's collection will get people's attention.

Conducting a survey enables the preservation officer to define the nature and extent of the problem in his or her institution. Thus far, the officer has responded well to the panic that has been stirred up. Now, all that has to be done is to formulate and implement a comprehensive plan that allows the institution to use the information gathered in the survey. It is embarrassingly easy to become bogged down at this point. The survey is so nice and finite, contained there in a paper file or on a computer disc, that one wants to believe it solves as well as defines the problem. Unfortunately, this is just not so.

Policy Statement

The institution will profit from creating a preservation policy statement that will provide a philosophical framework from which to proceed. A statement of the institution's preservation philosophy might include the definition of terms as they will be used in that setting, a statement of priorities for the preservation program, and an articulation of the duties of the various sections of the preservation program and the standards the staff of each section will follow in carrying out their responsibilities.

In order for a preservation program to succeed, the institutional philosophy as articulated in the policy statement must have broad-based support from all staff at all levels of the organization. It is not enough that an enthusiastic few develop the policy and support the goals of the program, since when these few retire, resign to take jobs elsewhere, or are promoted or transferred to another part of the organization where they cannot continue actively to support preservation, the very real danger exists that any impetus for the preservation program will die out among remaining staff.

It goes without saying that the program must have support from the top of the organization. The senior administrators not only set the course of the institution, but also set the tone of the institution by their words, actions, and tacit approval or disapproval of activities in that institution. A pragmatic approach is probably the best one for the head of the preservation program to take if he or she has any say in deciding where that program should report. It is useful to have preservation located in the most effective area of the institution, reporting to the most sympathetic and influential administrator. The results of the collection survey, including not only the hard data but also the reactions those data elicit throughout the organization, may suggest where in the organization a preservation effort belongs by identifying the area in which the most concentrated action is needed and welcomed.

PROSPECTIVE AND RETROSPECTIVE PRESERVATION

Roughly speaking, preservation action can be divided into two categories: prospective and retrospective preservation. By *prospective preservation* is meant actions that are taken to prevent or slow down the deterioration of or damage to library materials. Prospective preservation includes such things as stabilizing the environment and maintaining it at acceptable levels, mounting an aggressive and wide-ranging program of staff and user education, standardizing care and handling procedures, establishing a policy on the exhibition and loan of materials, and putting in place a collections maintenance program.

Prospective preservation tends to affect the greatest number of items at the same time. Thus the cost per item is low. This does not mean, however, that a program of prospective preservation is always free or even inexpensive to start up and maintain. However, since it is cost effective, it is often the logical place to begin any preservation action. Because prospective preservation tends to affect the greatest number of items, it also affects the greatest number of people. Therefore, it is essential to win the hearts and minds of as many people as possible, as early on as possible.

Retrospective preservation action is taken to counteract the effects of time, use, and the inherent physical problems of materials. It includes such actions as the conservation or restoration of individual items, the replacement of items that cannot or should not be used in their original format, and reformatting deteriorated material into another, more stable medium. Retrospective preservation tends to look at and then treat one item, or a batch of similar items, at a time. The cost per item, then, is relatively high.

Before proceeding any further, an explanation of terminology might be useful. *Preservation* is a broad term encompassing actions that anticipate, prevent, stop, or slow the deterioration of materials. *Conservation* is a narrower term, encompassing actions taken to maintain items in usable conditions. *Restoration* is narrower still, and describes actions taken to return a deteriorated item to original or near-original condition.

Returning to the concept of prospective preservation and to the fact that it affects a large number of items at the same time, it is often said that the best thing can be done for a collection is to control the environment in which it is kept. *Environment* here is used very broadly, and refers to temperature, humidity, and light; type of shelving and housing; physical maintenance of the stacks or storage area; and housekeeping practices. It is important to control these factors to the greatest degree possible, in order to derive the greatest benefit for the collection.

The importance of storage conditions is easily recognized when one considers that most materials spend most of their useful lives (and then, unfortunately, their unusable lives) sitting on a storage shelf. In the case of museum objects, that life may be spent on display. The embrittlement and deterioration of organic materials are chemical reactions, and the rate of every chemical reaction doubles for every 18°F increase in temperature. Taken together, those statements mean that, all else being equal, the collection stored at 78°F will deteriorate twice as fast as the collection stored at 60°F.

Logically speaking, the energy costs of keeping a library, archive, or museum at 60°F would be enormous; the psychological toll of listening to all user and staff complaints would be even greater. For these reasons, senior administrators are not likely to support an argument for such drastic measures. One should argue, then, for reasonable compromises in temperature and humidity controls in both public access and staff working areas. If an institution has storage/shelving areas to which access is restricted, one may argue for stricter environmental control in those parts of the building.

The preservation officer should also argue for controlling the amount and type of light that falls upon material in the collections, as light is damaging to nearly all types of collections. Sunlight, incandescent, and fluorescent light will bleach cloth, paper, and pigments; all contain ultraviolet radiation, which hastens chemical reactions harmful to paper and to cloth. Of the three, incandescent light is the least harmful. Incandescent light is also more expensive than fluorescent, which explains the widespread use of fluorescent light fixtures. Here, then, the compromise argument favors the purchase of devices which filter ultraviolet (UV) radiation, such as coating on windows and plastic sleeves that slip around fluorescent lighting tubes. One should also emphasize the importance of turning off the lights in any stack or storage area when it is not in use, whenever this can be done without compromising the safety of staff and users.

Establishing and maintaining a good environment is extremely important. It is also important to define, establish, and maintain good shelving and housing standards. The correct storage of materials enhances their useful life by providing the right kind and size of shelving, by providing work space within the storage area to examine materials removed from the shelves (especially important in the case of large or unwieldy items), and by providing adequate support for the material in the form of bookends or upright shelf dividers. Any housing system should be suited to the materials and nondamaging to them. Housing here means any boxes or other protective enclosure, reels, or spools for film, and closure devices. It will often fall to the preservation officer to identify and document incorrect storage/shelving practices, suggest modified or new practices, search for a supplier of appropriate furniture and housing devices, and train staff to work in the new environment.

A popular issue in librarianship these days is how to handle what is sometimes called "mixed media" or "items with accompanying material"; for example, a bound—or worse, a paperback book—that is issued with a map, computer disc, small board game, audiocassette, or whatever, in a pocket in the back of the book. Increasingly, the nonbook item is becoming the primary item and the text is the accompaniment, as, for example, a computer software program with its documentation. The questions of shelving and access are thorny ones whose answers impact both the preservation of and access to the material. Will a cassette be stolen if shelved in an open stack in a library? If the answer is yes, some other way to store the material must be found. Will the electronic information encoded on tape or disc be destroyed or hopelessly scrambled if the cassette or disc gets too close to a working magnetizer/demagnetizer used with some security systems? If the answer is yes, some other way to store the material must be found, or some way must be devised to clearly mark the book or storage container that houses the vulnerable material. Some institutions have opted for completely integrated shelving (books, records, tapes, etc., all shelved in one call number order); some have opted for shelving the entire package—book and accompanying material—in the collection or area of the collection that has the equipment necessary to access the nonbook medium; sadly, some libraries have taken the path of least resistance and locked up the material in an office somewhere where the user cannot get at it, if, indeed, the user can even discover that the library owns the material.

Maintaining a good working relationship with the housekeeping staff is an important part of prospective preservation. It is, after all, these staff members who are charged with the daily responsibility for cleaning the building that houses the collection. Rich rewards will come from the time and effort devoted to working with the housekeeping staff and explaining to them the importance of keeping the facilities as clean as possible. The reward comes the next time a staff member is in a remote corner of the collection area and notices something out of the ordinary—a small puddle of water on the floor or a water stain on the ceiling—and reports it to the preservation officer; or the next time the floor is stripped, washed, and rewaxed and not one drop splashes onto the lowest shelf. Worrying about housekeeping may not be the glamorous part of a preservation manager's job, but it is certainly a necessary one.

A strong, consistent, and realistic program of staff and user education will help in the effort to preserve the collections. The way in which each item is used and handled has a profound and direct impact on its longevity. Every staff member, from the mail room clerk to the senior administrator, should know how to handle correctly an item from the collection. Just as important, everyone should know why it is important to do so. Incorrect or careless handling can be structurally damaging and can shorten the life of the material. This being the case, incorrect or careless handling is a harmful and expensive habit. However, it is a habit that can be changed with a staff education program that first explains why material should be handled carefully and then goes on to train staff in correct techniques.

Presentations by preservation staff should be included in any orientation program for new staff. Some institutions have formal orientation programs that take place on an annual cycle, arranged and publicized through the personnel office. In this case, it will be fairly easy to work with the staff in personnel to put preservation in the orientation loop. If there is no formal orientation program to tie into, preservation staff will have to take a more active role, not only in designing and implementing the presentation itself, but also in making the arrangements. By its very nature, preservation tends to affect a broad range of institutional activities. Therefore, all staff should be made aware of current institutional preservation policies and activities and should be encouraged to contribute to the preservation effort by bringing their concerns and questions to the preservation staff. Responding to these concerns may require an increased level of day-to-day public relations effort, but the payoff is a greater level of staff engagement in collection preservation issues, problems, and solutions.

The message must be taken to the user of the collection or patron of the museum, too. This can be a far more difficult proposition than is that of educating staff. For instance, the preservation staff cannot control the public's use of materials checked out of a library. Neither can the staff control the public's use of materials inside the library or archive, unless there is a staff member working directly and continually with each patron. Realistically, this is not going to happen except in the case of the truly exceptional item. In the case of museums, there is the whole museum, one-of-a-kind mindset that makes most people (for the most part) obey the signs that say "Do not touch." Even then, museums are not totally exempt from patron misuse.

It is necessary to send the message to the patron by whatever means are at the institution's disposal. An exhibit that features some of the problems faced in the effort to preserve the collection and presents some of the solutions to those problems, is a good way to start raising the collective consciousness. Patron education can be looked at as an ongoing and, to be realistic, never-ending public relations campaign. Exhibits, handouts, bookmarks, and demonstrations of preservation problems and solutions can all be used effectively to make patrons more aware of their role in both the cause and solution to those problems.

A comprehensive and comprehensible disaster preparedness and recovery plan is an essential part of any preservation plan. It should be established early on in the institution's planning effort and should be revised and updated annually. One must plan carefully to prevent a disaster and also to cope with one. A general plan is useful to outline; for example, one should turn off the water, call the head of building services at the following number, contact the local business that agreed to loan the institution freezer space, etc. A specific plan is essential to lay out procedures for a particular unit; it is necessary to decide in advance what constitutes the most important part of the collection and to save it first. This prioritization of unit-level salvage operations should be based on value (by virtue of rarity or institutional association) and on the format of the material.

Yet, no matter how carefully an institution has thought out its program for prospective preservation action, it will eventually have to plan for, implement, and manage a program for the retrospective treatment of its collection. The line between prospective and retrospective preservation actions is not a distinct one. Although conservation was earlier classed as a retrospective activity, this is not always the case. Many conservation treatment options are used in two ways: to protect the item or prepare it for use or display (prospective preservation actions), and to treat the item in order to return it to usable or displayable condition (retrospective actions).

The treatment of materials from the collection can be an expensive proposition. Trained staff, the necessary equipment, and archival-quality supplies are all essential. However, they can be difficult to locate and more costly than untrained staff, jury-rigged equipment, and supplies that do not meet accepted archival standards. In the long run, going the quality route is worth the effort and investment, since correct treatment of material will enhance its stability, longevity, and usability. Moreover, since many institutions already carry out a program of item-level treatment with in-house repair programs, resources may have already been allocated and may already be available for the spending. The preservation manager, then, need only spend those resources wisely and well. Libraries that traditionally have had a budget for the commercial binding of books are in an enviable position in this regard. If the manager can achieve economies in the binding program, she or he may well be able to redirect the freed-up portion of the budget to other areas of the emerging preservation program.

Those institutions that have ongoing programs of in-house treatment of material may well decide to continue these activities, changing procedures and materials used, where appropriate, to bring the program to archival standard. Institutions that do not have established treatment programs face the decision of whether or not to begin such an effort. They might decide to carry out in-house treatment only on materials up to a certain designated level or value or that require a certain level of skill to perform the treatments. That is, in-house treatments may be performed by technicians on material that is not rare, unique, or above a dollar value set by the institution.

Not every institution need set up its own unit to do the expensive, time-consuming conservation and restoration work associated with rare materials and unique artifacts. Those services may be purchased from one of several sources—from a regional conservation center, or from private conservators, for example. Some library binders have or are establishing conservation units for the treatment of rare items and are offering a wide range of services to the library community. While these services are aimed primarily at treatment of bound materials, they do include such things as item-level and batch deacidification, and the construction of custom-made protective enclosures—services that also may apply to the archive and the museum community. On the other hand, the institution may decide at the outset or somewhere down the road that it will fund a unit capable of working on rare, valuable, and unique material. The preservation manager will doubtless be asked to justify the need for a more intense conservation component in the overall preservation program.

Many institutions find it helpful to join with like institutions in cooperative efforts to solve the problems associated with the preservation of collections. The opportunities for cooperative action should be taken into account when planning an institutional approach to preservation.

CONCLUSION

For those citizens concerned with preservation, the growing activity in the field is reassuring. It suggests that institutions recognize the issues, problems, and opportunities associated with the preservation of their collections, and that managers are grappling with the solutions to those problems. It does not suggest, and should not be taken to suggest, that the problems are solved. Perhaps the time for panic is past, but still needed are enthusiasm, commitment, and lots of hard work. It is exciting and rewarding work in which everyone can participate.

CONTRIBUTORS

SUSAN DALTON, Director of Preservation & Archival Projects, joined the National Center for Film and Video Preservation in 1987. Prior to this, she was associated with the Wisconsin Center for Film and Theater Research for ten years, first as archivisit and then as Associate Director. She holds a bachelor's degree in history from the University of Wisconsin-Madison and is the author of a number of articles on film history and former co-editor of *The Velvet Light Trap.*

GERALD D. GIBSON is curator of audio, film, and video in the Motin Picture, Broadcasting, and Recorded Sound Division of the Library of Congress. He holds master's degrees in library science from Syracuse University and in musicology from the Eastman School of Music. He is President of the International Association of Sound Archives and has consulted on audiovisual media for the Edison National Historic Site, the Italian Minister per i Beni Culturali (Rome), the Louisiana State Museum in New Orleans, and the National Archives and Records Administration (NARAS).

SARA WOLF GREEN has been Conservator at The Textile Museum since January 1988. She completed her M.A. in special studies (ethnographic and archaeological conservation) at George Washington University in 1976 and has worked in the conservation field since that time at the Smithsonian Institution, the Fiji Museum, and Texas Memorial Museum at the University of Texas at Austin. Ms. Green is a Fellow of the American Institute for Conservation of Historic and Artistic Works and is widely published in the areas of ethnographic and textile conservation.

KATHRYN LUTHER HENDERSON, Professor, Graduate School of Library and Information Science, University of Illinois at Urbana-Champaign, has been teaching courses in cataloging, classification, bibliographic organization, and technical services for twenty-five years. Recently, with William T Henderson, she has developed a course in the preservation of library materials. No stranger to Allerton Institute conferences, she has chaired two previous conferences and co-chaired, with William T Henderson, the predecessor to this conference: *Conserving and Preserving Library Materials* (1981).

WILLIAM T HENDERSON is Preservation Librarian and Associate Professor of Library Administration in the University of Illinois at Urbana-Champaign. For more than twenty-five years he has worked on a system-wide basis with binding and preservation in a large university library. He has incorporated preservation considerations and requirements into the Library's binding contracts and procedures and has been instrumental in developing a local in-house mending and repair facility into a conservation facility. He is a member of the Library's Preservation Committee; he has been consultant for other institutions and agencies on the development of preservation methods and programs; and, with Kathryn Luther Henderson, teaches an annual course in the Graduate School of Library and Information Science on Preservation of Library Materials. He has made presentations before the 1969 and 1981 Allerton Institute conferences.

KLAUS B. HENDRIKS is Director of the Conservation Research Division of the National Archives of Canada. His interests include management of technical service to libraries and archives and preservation of both paper and nonpaper materials. Dr. Hendriks holds a Ph.D. in organic chemistry from the University of Alberta. His accomplishments include specialized techniques for duplication of negatives and copying of prints, studies on the mechanism of silver image deterioration, and methods for restoration of faded or discolored photographs. He serves on ANSI subcommittees concerned with testing and storage of contemporary photographic records. Dr. Hendricks has lectured extensively on the preservation of archival records, and he has been consultant to UNESCO and to libraries and archives in many countries.

DENNIS INCH is Vice-President of Light Impressions, Inc., in Rochester, New York. Light Impressions is a major supplier of materials used in the conservation of photographic collections.

MARY L. LARSGAARD is the Assistant Head of the Map and Imagery Laboratory, University Library, University of California at Santa Barbara. She has master's degrees in library science and in geography. She is the author of *Map Librarianship, An Introduction*, now in its second edition (1987).

CARLA J. MONTORI is Head of the Preservation Division of the University of Michigan Library and Adjunct Lecturer in the School of Library and Information Studies. She holds a master's degree in library science from the Southern Connecticut State University. She is active in state, regional, and national preservation organizations, and is currently Vice-President of the Board of Directors of the Michigan Alliance for the Conservation of Cultural Heritage.

GORDON B. NEAVILL is Associate Professor in the School of Library and Information Studies at the University of Alabama in Tuscaloosa. He received his Ph.D. from the University of Chicago Graduate Library School. His research interests include the intellectual implications of electronic publishing and the history of the Modern Library series. He currently teaches courses in bibliographic organization and control, history of the book, modern book publishing,and a doctoral seminar in the sociology of knowledge.

MARY LYNN RITZENTHALER is Supervisory Conservator at the National Archives and Records Administration in Washington, D. C. Her publications include *Archives & Manuscripts, Conservation: A Manual on Physical Care and Management* (Society of American Archivists, 1983); *80 Years Later: 80th Anniversary Exhibition of the Guild of Book Workers* (The Guild, 1986); and *Preservation of Archival Records: Holdings Maintenance at the National Archives* (NARA, 1990).

SUSAN GARRETSON SWARTZBURG, Preservation Librarian, Rutgers University, has been involved with the preservation of newspapers for over sixteen years. She teaches courses on the Preservation of Library Materials and the History of Books and Printing at Rutgers School of Communication, Information and Library Studies. Author and columnist, her most recent book is *The Design and Renovation of Libraries and Archives from a Preservation Perspective* (Scarecrow Press, 1989). She is currently Associate Editor for News for *Conservation Administration News*.

LAMBERTUS VAN ZELST is Director of the Smithsonian Institution's Conservation Analytical Laboratory. After receiving his Ph.D. in nuclear chemistry, he worked at Brookhaven National Laboratory, the Metropolitan Museum of Art, and the Museum of Fine Arts, Boston. At the Smithsonian Institution, he is responsible for managing a laboratory for research and training in conservation, analysis and technical studies of museum objects and related materials.

HENRY WILHELM, Director of Research for the Preservatioin Publishing Company, is one of the original members of the American National Standards Institute subcommittee established in 1978 to write the now-completed ANSI IT9.9-1990 standard on test methods for measuring the stability of color photographs. Mr. Wilhelm served as technical advisor to film director Martin Scorsese in his successful campaign to persuade Kodak, Fuji, and Agfa-Gevaert to improve the stability of their color motion picture films. In an article written with Bob Schwalberg and Carol Brower in the June 1990 issue of *Popular Photography,* Mr. Wilhelm published comprehensive data on the light fading and dark storage stability of current color films and color print materials. A book by Wilhelm and contributing author Carol Brower, *The Permanence and Care of Color Photographs,* will be published by Preservation in 1991.

INDEX